DEATH GRIP

 *The Hoover Institution gratefully acknowledges*
Paul H. and Elisabeth E. Bauer
for their significant support of this publication.

DEATH GRIP

Loosening the Law's Stranglehold over Economic Liberty

CLINT BOLICK

HOOVER INSTITUTION PRESS
STANFORD UNIVERSITY | STANFORD, CALIFORNIA

www.hoover.org

Hoover Institution Press Publication No. 606

Hoover Institution at Leland Stanford Junior University, Stanford, California 94305-6010

First printing 2011
17 16 15 14 13 12 11   7 6 5 4 3 2 1

Manufactured in the United States of America

The paper used in this publication meets the minimum Requirements of the American National Standard for Information Sciences—Permanence of Paper for Printed Library Materials, ANSI/NISO Z39.48-1992. ∞

Cataloging-in-Publication Data is available from the Library of Congress.
ISBN-13: 978-0-8179-1314-4 (cloth. : alk. paper)
ISBN-13: 978-0-8179-1316-8 (e-book)

For Milton Friedman and Bernie Siegan,
two titans in the quest for economic liberty,
with gratitude for their friendship and enduring inspiration.

▌CONTENTS

INTRODUCTION AND ACKNOWLEDGMENTS

HERE'S A CIVICS STUMPER for you: can you name the three protections provided by the Fourteenth Amendment? Most Americans likely could not identify any of them without additional prompting. But even among people who are possessed of substantial civic knowledge, I'd wager the vast majority could name only two: due process of law and equal protection under the law. They're pretty famous. Even those who don't know they are part of the Fourteenth Amendment are likely to recognize the terms and know that they are important constitutional rights Americans possess.

It's the Fourteenth Amendment's remaining protection that would completely stump most Americans, even if it were listed among multiple-choice options: it's the guarantee that states may not abridge the privileges or immunities of citizens of the United States. If you asked the typical person on the street—indeed, even the typical lawyer—where the provision comes from or what it means, most wouldn't have a clue.

How could two of the three provisions of the Fourteenth Amendment be so well-known while the other is so obscure? Especially when they appear within the same sentence? Deepening the mystery, the privileges or immunities clause is listed *first* among the trilogy of

Fourteenth Amendment protections, suggesting that those who wrote it intended that the provision meant something important. Moreover, among the three protections, it is the only one that on its face protects *substantive* rights—that is, "privileges or immunities" that states may not abridge. By contrast, the other provisions on their face do not impose substantive limits on government power, but rather instruct that states may not infringe upon life, liberty, or property "without due process" and that they are bound to provide all individuals with equal protection of the laws.

The reason why Americans are familiar with due process and equal protection is that scores of court decisions have struck down laws as violations of those guarantees—including some of the most-famous cases of all time, such as *Brown v. Board of Education* and *Roe v. Wade.* Law students spend months studying those two provisions, and they are a core focus of the Constitutional Law portion of the bar examination.

By contrast, cases involving the privileges or immunities clause are exceedingly rare and are almost never in the news. As a result, most law students spend a minute or two, if that, studying about the privileges or immunities clause. In fact, they are taught to forget it exists. Indeed, when I was studying for the California bar examination, the instructor told the students that there was only one thing they needed to know about the privileges or immunities clause: that it is *never* the correct answer to a bar exam question.

How did such a seminal constitutional provision plummet to such jurisprudential depths? Most legal questions have complex answers—or at least lawyers who charge by the hour want you to think that they do—but the answer to this one is easy. Only a few years after the Fourteenth Amendment was enacted following the close of the Civil War, the U.S. Supreme Court drained the privileges or immunities clause of nearly all its meaning in one of the worst decisions in the history of American law, the aptly named *Slaughter-House Cases.*[1]

In that 1873 decision, the Supreme Court by a 5–4 vote—highly unusual in those days—upheld a bribery-procured Louisiana slaughter-house monopoly that had been challenged by a group of butchers whose businesses were jeopardized. In that decision, the court discovered a new way to amend the Constitution: by judicial fiat. The majority ruled that the privileges or immunities clause added almost nothing to the handful of rights protected against abuse by the states in the original Constitution. By that decision, one of the most important and beneficial products of the Civil War—a revolutionary constitutional provision intended to protect civil rights against oppression by state governments—was nullified. So while myriad cases since the Fourteenth Amendment was adopted have invoked the equal protection and due process clauses, until recently not a single U.S. Supreme Court decision invoked the privileges or immunities clause to strike down a law.

The *Slaughter-House Cases* produced many unfortunate consequences, several of which will be discussed in the pages that follow. But foremost among them was the evisceration of one of the most sacred and central rights of Americans: economic liberty, the right to pursue a business or occupation free from arbitrary or excessive government regulation. Now, nearly a century and a half later, this right that many Americans deem fundamental enjoys virtually no legal protection whatsoever. If the government tries to take away someone's welfare check, a Legal Services Corporation lawyer (your taxpayer dollars at work) can tie the government up in knots. But if the government decides to regulate your business out of existence—even for the benefit of a competitor—you have virtually no constitutional recourse.

This state of affairs is particularly devastating for people at the bottom rungs of the economic ladder. The most pernicious regulatory barriers to opportunity are those that restrict entry into businesses and occupations that require little formal education or capital. Those regulations hinder meaningful participation in the mainstream economy, as well as upward economic mobility, to millions of economically disadvantaged Americans. At the same time, they limit market entry and inhibit competition at every level of the economy, as sophisticated business or labor interests manipulate government power to protect and enhance their economic positions to the detriment of others.

The privileges or immunities clause was intended to provide legal recourse to individuals affected by such laws. But the clause was killed in its infancy. That is a perversion of American law. The time has come to correct it—to restore economic liberty to its rightful place among the most fundamental civil rights.

The conditions for change may be ripe. Legal scholars on both sides of the philosophical spectrum have condemned the *Slaughter-House Cases*. Moreover, a majority of members of the current U.S. Supreme Court adhere to a philosophy of "original intent," which opens them to arguments based on the intent of the Constitution's framers.

But it is a difficult task to overturn a longstanding precedent, even if it is obviously wrong. In particular, some conservative judges and scholars fear that breathing life into the privileges or immunities clause would open a Pandora's box of judicial adventurism. Yet that fear is nothing compared to the real-world harm inflicted upon Americans whose economic liberty is denied by government.

In 1984, Judge (now Justice) Antonin Scalia debated libertarian law professor Richard Epstein on this very topic at the Cato Institute. Scalia argued that it was premature to consider restoring judicial protection for economic liberty; important groundwork first must be laid. "[T]he task of creating what I might call a constitutional ethos of economic liberty is no easy one," he warned. "But it is the first task."[2]

I took Scalia's words as a clarion call. As a young lawyer only a few years out of law school, I set myself on a goal so audaciously hopeful that it would make Barack Obama proud (if he liked free enterprise): to overturn the *Slaughter-House Cases*. With the encouragement of my boss and mentor—the chairman of the U.S. Equal Employment Opportunity Commission, Clarence Thomas, who would go on to become an associate justice of the United States Supreme Court—I wrote a book called *Changing Course* that sketched out the idea. Even though hardly anyone read the book, the idea was interesting enough to the Lynde and Harry Bradley Foundation to provide a seed grant to Landmark Legal Foundation to put me to work. And the quest to overturn *Slaughter-House* and restore economic liberty as a fundamental civil right began in earnest.

Since that time, I have had the great privilege and opportunity to litigate many economic liberty cases (several of them described in Part 4) at the Institute for Justice, which I co-founded in 1990, and since 2007 at the Goldwater Institute in Phoenix. It has been gratifying to see talented attorneys such as Clark Neily at the Institute for Justice and Timothy Sandefur at Pacific Legal Foundation take on this task as well. We still have a long way to go, but our successes so far in the courts of law and the court of public opinion suggest that we are doing something more than tilting at windmills. Ultimately, our goal is to convince the U.S. Supreme Court to revisit the *Slaughter-House Cases* and to invest the privileges or immunities clause with the meaning intended by its framers.

The four parts of this book proceed as follows. In part 1, I sketch the sorry state of economic liberty in the nation that stands as a beacon of opportunity to the rest of the world. In part 2, I examine the history and intent of the Fourteenth Amendment and the judicial nullification of the privileges or immunities clause in the *Slaughter-House Cases*. Part 3 examines the horrible aftermath of *Slaughter-House*, whose tragic consequences continue to manifest themselves today. For readers who slog through those three depressing sections, the payoff is part 4, which describes the campaign to restore economic liberty as a fundamental civil right, so far with limited but growing success.

I am enormously grateful to the many people who have seen fit over the years to support this work. It seems to me that the principal debt we as Americans owe to future generations is to leave our nation at least as free as we found it. And the promise of opportunity is the cornerstone of the freedom on which our nation's moral claim is staked.

I am privileged to pursue this work at the Goldwater Institute, named after one of the all-time greatest stalwarts for freedom. Sustained by a devoted board of directors and generous supporters who are just as devoted to freedom as Senator Barry Goldwater was, this mission is advanced by a talented and dedicated staff including the Institute's president, Darcy Olsen, and my fellow litigators: Nick Dranias, Carrie Ann Sitren, Diane Cohen, Christina Kohn, and Gustavo Schneider.

I am very grateful as well to the Hoover Institution, which I serve as a research fellow, for its tremendous scholarship, for its exceptionally well-informed supporters who exert positive influence in many areas of public policy, and specifically for the chance to tell a story that is unfamiliar to many of my fellow advocates of freedom: the story of the demise and rebirth of economic liberty in America. It is a story that began with great promise, beckoning countless new Americans to our shores with the lure of limitless opportunity, resulting in the richest and greatest nation on Earth. Yet the promise fell prey to tragic errors that we need to correct today, lest we sacrifice the opportunity that ought to be every American's birthright. I hope that with persistence and dedication, the story will have an ending that is happily ever after.

In the process of telling this story, I hope not only to help nudge jurisprudence in the right direction but to inspire others to take up or support the cause. There is no richer or more important legacy we can leave to future generations of Americans than true and enduring freedom of enterprise.

—Phoenix, Arizona
August 2010

PART 1

THE SORRY STATE OF ECONOMIC LIBERTY

IN ONE OF THE FIRST economic liberty cases I argued, the judge lamented that the oppressive regulatory barriers that my clients faced sounded more like Russia than the United States. I replied that in fact we might have to seek economic asylum for our clients in Russia, because these days there are fewer barriers to entry in Russia than in our country. The judge laughed ruefully. And then, shortly thereafter, he ruled against us—not because he wanted to, but because the weight of case law against economic liberty was too great.

Such was the state of economic liberty jurisprudence as we entered the millennium. Economic rights are consigned to the lowest level of judicial scrutiny—the so-called "rational basis" test. As most courts have applied it to economic regulations over the past eighty years, there are two features to the rational basis test. First, the regulation doesn't have to be rational. Second, it doesn't have to have a basis.

It's not much of a test, and almost no contested regulations ever flunk it. As a consequence, law students are taught that when the rational basis test applies to a particular controversy between an individual and the government, the government always wins.

Leroy Jones had never heard about the rational basis test, much less the privileges or immunities clause, when the government tried to destroy his dream in the early 1990s. Jones was a cab driver in Denver, working for the ubiquitous Yellow Cabs. He and some of his fellow drivers noticed an oddity in the Denver taxicab market. Cabs were abundant at downtown hotels and the airport. But if someone needed a cab in the low-income Five Points neighborhood, it was tough to get one.

Jones and three of his colleagues saw opportunity in this. They decided to form a new taxicab cooperative, named Quick-Pick Cabs, that would primarily serve Five Points and other taxicab-scarce neighborhoods. They already possessed the requisite experience. They assembled the necessary capital. They collected hundreds of signatures from Five Points residents attesting to the need for additional taxicab service.

Indeed, the aspiring entrepreneurs had everything they needed to launch a profitable enterprise that would provide a valuable service—everything, that is, except for a piece of paper from the Colorado Public Utilities Commission called a "certificate of public convenience and necessity." No problem, reasoned Jones and his colleagues—their business was both convenient and necessary. But after the agency completed its review, it delivered to Quick-Pick Cabs the same verdict as every other applicant for a taxicab permit since World War II: application denied.

It turned out that the rules of the game were rigged decisively in favor of the three existing taxicab companies. A new applicant had the burden of showing not that there was a market need that was unserved, but that there was a need that *could not be met* by the existing companies. It was an impossible burden, exacerbated by the fact that the existing companies could intervene in the proceedings and literally bleed their aspiring competitor to death with massive and endless documentation demands.

Jones and his partners were denied the opportunity to pursue their business for the most arbitrary and protectionist reasons. One could hardly imagine a greater injustice. Yet when they went to federal court, they lost. Once again, there simply was not enough case law for the judge to render a favorable ruling. Having now been fired from Yellow Cabs, Leroy Jones ended up selling cold drinks under the hot sun at Mile High Stadium, his dream of starting his own company crushed by his own local government. (Lest the reader get too depressed, this story has a happy ending—but I won't reveal it until later.)

Most of the stories in similar circumstances, however, do not have happy endings. One of the saddest and most frustrating cases I ever litigated was on behalf of Junie Allick, a native Virgin Islands sailor. He made a living shuttling tourists to the beautiful coral reef at Buck Island. He was the only sailor in the business skillful enough to operate only with sails, as opposed to the gasoline engines that polluted the reef. But after the National Park Service assumed jurisdiction over Buck Island, it instituted an "attrition" policy to reduce the number of boat trips to Buck Island. For the first time, Allick had to navigate not only the waters off St. Croix but a sea of bureaucracy as well. Though Allick was a skilled sailor, he had never learned to read or write, and he failed to fill out forms required by the Park Service, which consequently shut his business down. Before long, not a single native sailor was left in the Buck Island excursion business.

Yet when we brought Allick's case to court, the federal judge was incredulous that someone would waste the court's time over a business that netted only $15,000 a year. He dismissed the case, thereby destroying the only livelihood Allick had ever known.

The barriers encountered by Leroy Jones and Junie Allick are only the tip of the regulatory iceberg. In all, at least five hundred occupations, representing 10 percent of all professions, require government licenses.[1] Frequently, the government boards that determine the standards are comprised of members of the regulated profession, who are invested with the coercive power of government and often wield it not for public health and safety purposes but to thwart competition. Similarly, government-imposed monopolies in businesses ranging from trash hauling to transportation to the transmission of renewable energy have the same effect.

The economist Walter Williams, in his classic book *The State Against Blacks*, explained that occupational licensing laws and entry-level business restrictions have the pernicious effect of removing the bottom rungs of the economic ladder for people who have little education and few resources. "The laws are not discriminatory in the sense that they are aimed specifically at blacks," he explains. "But they are discriminatory in the sense that they deny full opportunity for the most disadvantaged Americans, among whom blacks are disproportionately represented."[2]

A good illustration of Williams's point was provided in Stuart Dorsey's study of Missouri's cosmetology licensing regime. Like most cosmetology licensing laws, Missouri's law requires a practical "hands-on" examination and a difficult written test. Dorsey found that blacks passed the performance portion of the examination at the same rate as whites, but failed the written portion at a much higher rate than whites. Thus were black candidates disproportionately excluded from a profession for which they were demonstrably qualified.[3] In an economy that demands ever-greater educational qualifications for even the most basic jobs, there simply are not nearly enough avenues for legitimate entry-level businesses or occupations to sustain arbitrary regulatory obstacles. Those hurdles cast otherwise legitimate businesses into the underground economy, and many of their would-be participants into crime or welfare dependency.

Lurking behind most of these regulatory obstacles are special interests—usually labor unions, competing businesses, or both—who invoke the regulatory power of the state to keep newcomers out. In New York, for instance, the powerful transit workers union manipulates the City Council to maintain a ban on dollar vans, which operate mainly in the underground economy to carry scores of passengers in Jamaica, Queens, over fixed routes for a low price. Frequently, professions turn to the state to fix high barriers to entry, then gain control over the licensing process. In the early part of the twentieth century, for instance, cosmetologists fought valiantly to free themselves from control by barber licensing boards—only to turn around, once they succeeded, to lobby for cosmetology licensing boards that they would control. Today, even professions that trigger few public health and safety concerns, such as interior designers, florists, and yoga instructors, seek shelter from marketplace competition through licensing schemes. As a consequence, government-enforced cartels now are abundant throughout the land.

Professions requiring more advanced skills, such as law and medicine, typically persuade lawmakers to forbid para-professionals, who offer their services at much lower cost, forcing them to become fully licensed even though they seek to engage only in a small specialized part of the profession. As a result, legislators penalize both the would-be para-professionals and the consumers who might wish to procure their services.

Perhaps the most troubling example in that regard is my own profession. Lawyers operate state bar associations that rigidly control entry into the profession. And they expansively define the unauthorized practice of law so as to prevent skilled paralegals from making low-cost legal services available to people for routine transactions such as tenant evictions, simple wills, divorce decrees, and bankruptcies. The arbitrary barriers raise the cost and limit the supply of the most basic legal services. Surely regulation is sufficient to weed out incompetent para-professionals, but the bar typically opts instead for prohibition, the better to protect its cartel.

Equally pernicious are teacher certification schemes. As a certified teacher, I can attest that none of my required classroom instruction (all of which was state-required) enhanced my core subject-matter competence. Despite the fact that they often turn out ill-trained teachers, schools of education fiercely defend their monopoly status over teacher certification, resisting alternative certification and entry into teacher ranks by professionals who are demonstrably competent in their subject matter. The scheme ensures that many bad teachers enter the school system while many good teachers are kept out.

Not only in the teaching profession, but in many others, licensing is not a proxy for competence. However, because licensing typically

requires many hours of prescribed training, it is an effective means
of limiting entry into professions. Licensing requirements are lucrative for schools that teach the prescribed courses, and insulate licensed practitioners from competition. But they result in higher
prices and fewer choices for consumers while destroying economic
opportunities.

Such special-interest legislation greatly concerned the framers of
our Constitution, who sought to prevent it. James Madison argued
in *The Federalist No. 10* that one of the strongest arguments for republican government is "its tendency to break and control the vio-
lence of faction." By "faction," Madison meant what today is called a
special-interest group: "a number of citizens, whether amounting to
a majority or minority of the whole, who are united and actuated by
some common impulse of passion, or of interest, adverse to the rights
of other citizens, or to the permanent and aggregate interests of the
community." One means to limit the evil of faction, Madison observed, would be to control its liberty of operation (as we see today
in the form of campaign contribution limits and other devices), but
Madison denounced such cures as worse than the disease. The better
course in dealing with the problem of faction, he offered, was "controlling its effects" by "rendering it unable to concert and carry into
effect schemes of oppression."

The constitutional mechanisms designed in part to control the evils
of faction were many, including the establishment of a federal government with limited and defined powers; the requirement that congressional action may be taken only to promote the general welfare;
separation of powers; an independent judiciary empowered to strike
down unconstitutional laws (as described by Alexander Hamilton in
The Federalist No. 78); specific limitations of government power such as
prohibiting the impairment of contracts; and the Bill of Rights, including the protection of unenumerated rights in the Ninth Amendment. Madison's argument also provided a philosophical foundation
for the privileges or immunities and equal protection guarantees of the
Fourteenth Amendment a century later.

Specifically, the framers understood that two of the principal objects of factions were to gain power over the property of others and to restrict their liberty. Thus the Fifth Amendment prohibited Congress from infringing liberty or property without due process of law and from using the power of eminent domain except for public use with just compensation. The Fifth Amendment's due process guarantee later would be replicated in the Fourteenth Amendment, aimed in that amendment at curbing the power of state governments.

One of the foremost liberties threatened by the evil of faction was economic liberty. As Timothy Sandefur explains in his recent book, *The Right to Earn a Living*, American law inherited from its British forebears the principle that "people have the right to work for their subsistence, to open their own businesses, and to compete against one another, without government's interceding to confer special benefits on political favorites."[4] Dating back to the sixteenth century, British courts refused to enforce monopolies because they violated rights granted by the Magna Carta. As Sir Edward Coke observed in *The Case of the Tailors of Ipswich* in 1615, "at the common law, no man could be prohibited from working in any lawful trade," and "the common law abhors all monopolies, which prohibit any from working in any lawful trade."[5]

Adam Smith likewise extolled the importance of freedom of enterprise in his *Wealth of Nations*:

> The property which every man has in his own labor . . . is the original foundation of all other property, so it is the most sacred and inviolable. The patrimony of the poor man lies in the strength and dexterity of his own hands; and to hinder him from employing this strength and dexterity in what manner he thinks proper, without injury to his neighbor, is a plain violation of this most sacred property. It is a manifest encroachment upon the just liberty both of the workman and of those who might be disposed to employ him. As it hinders the one from working at what he thinks proper, so it hinders the others from employing whom they think proper.[6]

Embracing that tradition, Thomas Jefferson wrote, "Every one has a natural right to choose for his pursuit such one of them as he thinks most likely to furnish him subsistence," and a "first principle" of rightful government is the "guarantee to every one of a free exercise of his industry, and the fruits acquired by it." Likewise, Madison declared, "That is not a just government, nor is property secure under it, where arbitrary restrictions, exemptions, and monopolies deny to part of its citizens that free use of their faculties, and free choice of their occupations."[7]

Those principles were embodied in the Virginia Declaration of Rights in 1776, which in turn influenced the Declaration of Independence and the Bill of Rights. The first article of the Virginia Declaration of Rights provides that "all men are by nature equally free and independent, and have certain inherent rights," which include "the enjoyment of life and liberty, with the means of acquiring and possessing property, and pursuing happiness and safety."

Economic liberty was expressly protected in the U.S. Constitution by such provisions as the due process clause, which protects life, liberty, and property; the contract clause, which forbids state interference with contracts; the privileges and immunities clause, which gives to anyone traveling to other states the same rights as citizens of those states; the commerce clause, which prohibits protectionist trade barriers among states; and the prohibition against the taking of property through eminent domain except for public uses. The right to pursue a trade or profession also was one of the "unenumerated rights" protected by the Ninth Amendment.

The promise of opportunity and its protection by the rule of law propelled American enterprise and made our nation a beacon of opportunity, luring to our shores countless newcomers hoping to earn a share of the American Dream. One would think that such principles would protect a man like Leroy Jones in pursuit of his livelihood. After all, the regulations he faced brought about a government-created taxicab oligopoly, closed to entry or competition from outsiders. It was procured and maintained by the existing companies, not for the protection of the public but for their own benefit. Those factors would place the regulations squarely within the crosshairs of the constitutional provisions designed to prevent special-interest groups from using government power to serve their interests through the erection of monopolies. And yet when he went to court to protect the freedom of enterprise that is every American's birthright, Jones came away empty-handed—just like countless other entrepreneurs who have unsuccessfully sought to invoke judicial protection for their economic liberty.

It is difficult to fully appreciate how completely eviscerated the right to economic liberty is today without considering relevant U.S. Supreme Court cases—three in particular. In the 1955 case of *Williamson v. Lee Optical*, the court sustained a statute prohibiting opticians from duplicating old or broken eyeglass lenses, or from fitting old lenses into new frames, without a prescription from a licensed optometrist. The challenged regulation stifled a legitimate business and raised costs to consumers—not to protect the public, but to insulate licensed optometrists from competition for lucrative services. Yet the court had no trouble sustaining it. In a decision by the self-styled champion of the common man, Justice William O. Douglas, the court ruled that even though the "law may exact a needless, wasteful requirement," it is "for the legislature, not the courts, to balance the advantages and disadvantages of the new requirement."[8]

What is perhaps the quintessential modern economic liberty decision came twenty-one years later in *City of New Orleans v. Dukes*. There the court was presented with a law that destroyed for many the classic entry-level enterprise: hot dog pushcarts. The plaintiff had operated her pushcart in the French Quarter for many years until the city decided to prohibit them—except for two vendors whose businesses were "grandfathered." The court of appeals found the prohibition totally arbitrary and irrational, and struck it down. But the Supreme Court sustained the law, declaring that "this Court consistently defers to legislative determinations as to the desirability of particular statutory discriminations."[9]

How complete this deference has become is illustrated in a more recent case, *FCC v. Beach Communications*, decided by a unanimous

Supreme Court in 1993. There the court considered a federal statute that subjected to regulation satellite master antenna television
(SMATV) operations that encompassed more than one property
owned by different people, but exempted such operations when they
were confined to buildings owned by the same owners. Because
SMATV does not use public rights-of-way, the court of appeals
could not discern any reason for Congress to draw the dividing line
where it did—and to inflict very divergent consequences based on
the distinction—so it struck the provision under the equal protection
clause. The Supreme Court overturned the court of appeals decision,
setting forth the extreme deference to administrative discretion in a
set of rules implementing the rational basis standard:

1. The court held that "equal protection is not a license for courts
   to judge the wisdom, fairness, or logic of legislative choices. In
   areas of social and economic policy, a statutory classification
   . . . must be upheld against equal protection challenge if
   there is any reasonably conceivable set of facts that could
   provide a rational basis for the classification."[10]
2. "On rational-basis review, a classification . . . comes to us
   bearing a strong presumption of validity, and those attacking
   the rationality of the legislative classification have the burden
   'to negative every conceivable basis which might support it'."[11]
3. "[E]qual protection 'does not demand for purposes of
   rational-basis review that a legislature or governing decision-
   maker actually articulate at any time the purpose or rationale
   supporting its classification'."[12]
4. Because the government does not have to articulate its rationale, "it is entirely irrelevant for constitutional purposes
   whether the conceived reason for the challenged distinction
   actually motivated the legislature."[13]
5. Finally, "a legislative choice is not subject to courtroom fact-
   finding and may be based on rational speculation unsupported
   by evidence or empirical data."[14]

Talk about an uphill battle! This is the nearly impossible burden litigators challenging economic regulations face when they go to court—and why the courts felt compelled to turn away the claims of Leroy Jones and Junie Allick.

The Court in *Beach Communications* referred to this standard as "a paradigm of judicial restraint."[15] But actually, it is an exemplar of judicial abdication. The framers of our republican system of government never intended the courts to blindly defer to legislative decision-making, especially where the challenged laws were procured to advantage special interests and exact a large toll on precious individual liberties. But decisions such as those discussed here have obliterated the constitutional protections the framers carefully crafted to arrest the evils of faction and to protect individual rights. As the framers understood, only the courts can effectively police the boundaries of legitimate government action. But decisions like these make legislators the judges of their own power, and too rarely do they act with restraint.

Even worse, many of the regulations are imposed not by elected representatives, who are at least theoretically accountable to the people, but by regulatory agencies that are not democratically accountable at all. Most such agencies either are comprised of members of the regulated industry or are susceptible to special-interest influence. Their cumbersome rule-making procedures are opaque and often mystifying to ordinary people. Yet the courts accord them the same vast deference as they give to elected representatives, no matter how irrational, self-serving, excessive, or oppressive their regulations may be.

Those who bear the burden of economic regulation rarely have the resources to compete effectively in the political marketplace or administrative arenas against powerful special-interest groups, and so their constitutional rights fall by the wayside. This fate has befallen economic liberty not because judges are consistently restrained in exercising their powers—after all, courts strike down laws every day. Rather, it is the result of judges relegating economic liberty to a subordinate, almost completely unprotected status compared to other rights that enjoy greater favor.

That was not at all the fate our Constitution's framers intended. The pages that follow demonstrate that economic liberty was intended to be protected among the foremost of our civil rights, and that an unfortunate long-ago decision of the U.S. Supreme Court heralded an era of judicial abdication that now has lasted nearly 140 years. But, more hopefully, they also show that the path toward reclaiming protection for freedom of enterprise finally is before us.

PART 2

▌ SLAUGHTER-HOUSE

AMERICA HAS EXPERIENCED two revolutions that have fundamentally influenced its organic law. The first was the war for independence, which culminated in the United States Constitution. The second was the Civil War, which culminated in the Thirteenth, Fourteenth, and Fifteenth Amendments to the Constitution.

In both of these periods, the framers were animated by profoundly revolutionary principles, specifically the principles of natural rights. Unlike any other two periods in American history, these years were notable because those principles were nearly universally shared by the men involved in constitutional draftsmanship. In the context of the Civil War amendments, that was the case because those who were vanquished during the war were excluded from the process of constitutional revision—though they were compelled to ratify those changes in exchange for readmitting their states as full participants in the Union. Professor Michael Kent Curtis, one of the leading scholars of the Fourteenth Amendment, notes that most of the Republicans who dominated the Reconstruction Congress "saw events from 1830 to 1866 as a battle between slavery and freedom, a battle to determine whether the nation would become all slave or all free."[1]

Having won on the battlefield and now in unquestioned control of Congress, they were determined to vindicate freedom.

Unlike the Thirteenth Amendment, which was adopted quickly to abolish slavery, the Fourteenth Amendment did not spring forth immediately from the Civil War. Rather, it emanated from experiences occurring in the war's aftermath. Though beaten in war, the southern states were not prepared to abandon their ways. In particular, they were determined to preserve the institution of slavery as closely as possible, in substance if not in form.

To do so, they enacted a series of laws called the "black codes," which were designed to maintain a servile labor supply among the newly emancipated blacks. Though they could not completely deprive blacks of political rights, through the black codes the southern states were able to accomplish economic subjugation. The laws deprived blacks of the basic tools for economic advancement: freedom of contract and private property rights. Specifically, the laws impeded the ability of blacks to freely bargain over the terms and conditions of employment or to engage in certain jobs or occupations. In his report to Congress on the condition of the South in 1865, Major General Carl Schurz observed that "opposition to the negro's controlling his own labor, carrying on independently on his own account—in one word, working for his own benefit—showed itself in a variety of ways," such as regulations "heavily taxing or otherwise impeding those trades and employments in which colored people are most likely to engage."[2]

The black codes provoked the Reconstruction Congress to protect the economic liberty of newly freed blacks. After recounting the severe restrictions placed upon contract rights in the South, Rep. Martin Thayer of Pennsylvania asked "what kind of freedom is that by which the man placed in a state of freedom is subject to the tyranny of laws which deprive him of rights which the humblest citizen in every State in Christendom enjoys . . . [such as] the liberty to engage in the ordinary pursuits of life?"[3] As Rep. William Lawrence of Ohio observed, it "is idle to say that a citizen shall have the right to life, yet to deny him the right to labor, whereby alone he can live."[4]

The first step was not a constitutional amendment but a federal statute. The Civil Rights Act of 1866 was designed to protect both substantive economic liberties and equal protection of the laws, establishing that all citizens

> have the same right [to] make and enforce contracts, to sue, be parties, and give evidence, to inherit, purchase, lease, sell, hold, and convey real and personal property, and to the full and equal benefit of all laws [for] the security of persons and property, as is enjoyed by white citizens, and shall be subject to like punishment, [and] to none other, any law . . . to the contrary notwithstanding.

Although the Civil Rights Act of 1866 embodied values of free enterprise that undergirded the American experiment from its inception, it represented a dramatic break with prior theories of constitutional government, and as a consequence it set off a political firestorm. When the original Constitution was established, it was intended that the powers of the national government would be few and the residual powers of the states would be many, in part because the national government was perceived to present the greater threat to freedom, and the states were viewed as reliable guardians of freedom. The intervening years turned that notion topsy-turvy. While states did resist the expansion of the powers of the national government, many of them also acted—through the institution of human slavery and related deprivations of liberty—in tyrannical ways. Thus, while there were constitutional mechanisms by which states could protect their citizens against the national government, there were few mechanisms by which people could protect their rights against state governments. Having fought and won a civil war against state oppression, the Reconstruction Congress was determined to prevent states from ever again denying the basic rights of people who resided within their borders.

As originally structured, the Constitution gave the national government few powers to protect people against the violation of individual rights by state governments. Courts hadn't yet, for instance, invented the notion that congressional power to regulate interstate commerce through substantive legislation was nearly boundless. Likewise, the protection of individual liberty in the Bill of Rights applied only to the *national* government, not state governments. That was a consequence of the grand compromise that led to the Constitution, in which states agreed to join the new nation only if their powers (including the power to sanction slavery) were not substantially curtailed. Rep. Thaddeus Stevens of Pennsylvania, one of the prime architects of the Fourteenth Amendment, sagely remarked that "[o]ur fathers had been compelled to postpone the principles of their great Declaration, and wait for their full establishment till a more propitious time."[5]

As a result, except in limited instances, citizens whose rights were violated by state governments could look only to state constitutions for protection and to state courts to enforce the guarantees—which in the case of newly emancipated blacks in the South following the Civil War often meant no protection at all. So the Civil Rights Act of 1866 was at once both necessary to protect the rights of southern blacks against oppressive state governments and an audacious departure from the traditional understanding of the respective powers of the national and state governments. Not surprisingly, those two factors tugged in opposite directions, at a time in which both the nature of rights and the constitutional bounds of government power dominated congressional debate.[6]

Not surprisingly, opponents argued that the Civil Rights Act of 1866 represented an unprecedented expansion of federal power and a betrayal of states' rights. But "[a]rguments by Democrats that the protection of fundamental rights would interfere with the legitimate rights of states struck Republicans as absurd," Curtis observes. "No state retained the legitimate authority to deprive citizens of their fundamental rights because government, at all levels, was designed to protect such rights."[7]

While Congress set aside misgivings about the extent of national power in enacting the Civil Rights Act of 1866, the law's constitutionality was in serious question. President Andrew Johnson vetoed the bill on that basis, and Congress enacted the law over his veto. But sufficient doubt existed to induce Congress to "constitutionalize" the Civil Rights Act of 1866 by amending the Constitution to make congressional power over civil rights explicit and to protect those rights against violation by the states.

The first draft of the Fourteenth Amendment, by Rep. John Bingham of Ohio, merely extended to Congress the power to protect the rights set forth.[8] As adopted, however, the first section of the Fourteenth Amendment was self-executing against the states:

> No State shall make or enforce any law which shall abridge the privileges or immunities of citizens of the United States; nor shall any State deprive any person of life, liberty, or property, without due process of law; nor deny to any person within its jurisdiction the equal protection of the laws.

The chosen language is noteworthy for many reasons, two of which are especially pertinent. First, the framers of the Fourteenth Amendment wrote in universal terms, using language that encompasses all citizens (with regard to privileges or immunities) and all persons (with regard to due process and equal protection). Although the principal object of the Civil Rights Act of 1866 had been protecting the rights of blacks, and universal language was used even in that law, here the framers were using all-encompassing terms to recognize and protect certain rights. Indeed, the language is reminiscent of the Declaration of Independence, which starts with the proclamation that all men are created equal and endowed with inalienable rights. Likewise, Curtis observes that one of the central themes invoked by the framers of the Fourteenth Amendment was "the need for 'irreversible guarantees of liberty,' which would secure protection for the 'rights of men—men of all classes and conditions'."[9] On its face, the Fourteenth Amendment protects those rights against state governments.

Second, the most important language appears (unsurprisingly) to be the first of the three provisions. The second and third provisions require government to apply due process when they deprive individuals of life, liberty, or property, and to provide equal protection of the laws, but they do not on their face protect substantive rights. By contrast, the first clause on its face places substantive constraints on the powers of the states and on the types of laws they may enact by prohibiting them from making or enforcing all laws that abridge privileges or immunities of citizens.

Plainly, the architects of the privileges or immunities clause meant to accomplish something consequential. But exactly what?

At the very least, most historians and legal scholars "agree on one point: the Privileges or Immunities Clause was meant to protect, in some fashion, the freedoms enumerated in the Civil Rights Act of 1866. Property and contract rights, access to the courts and personal security were the principal concerns of the Act."[10] Beyond that, Professor Kimberly C. Shankman and the Cato Institute's director of constitutional studies, Roger Pilon, argue that "not only was the clause meant to be the centerpiece of section 1 of the Fourteenth Amendment; more important, it was meant to be a reflection of the underlying theory of the original Constitution and a link to the natural rights principles of the Declaration of Independence that form the intellectual foundation of American constitutionalism."[11]

An examination of the legislative history supports that broad reading. Though the term "privileges or immunities" is not part of the modern civic lexicon, to the Fourteenth Amendment's framers it had a clear meaning. Curtis notes that the terms "privileges" and "immunities" were a "shorthand description of fundamental or constitutional rights." That use of the terms "had a long and distinguished heritage," he writes. For instance, "Blackstone's *Commentaries on the Laws of England*, published in the colonies on the eve of the Revolution, had divided the rights and liberties of English men into those 'immunities' that were the residuum of natural liberties and those 'privileges' that society had provided in lieu of natural rights."[12]

As Justice Clarence Thomas recently observed, "At the time of Reconstruction, the term 'privileges' and 'immunities' had an established meaning as synonyms for 'rights'."[13] The term exists in the original Constitution: Article IV, section 2 provides that the "Citizens of each State shall be entitled to all Privileges and Immunities of Citizens in the several States." As Thomas explains, the framers of the Fourteenth Amendment understood that provision to prohibit states "from discriminating against sojourning citizens when recognizing fundamental rights, but did not require States to recognize those rights and did not prescribe their content."[14]

With the ratification of the Fourteenth Amendment on July 20, 1868, both of those limitations were erased: states were required to protect their own citizens' fundamental rights and the amendment gave those rights substantive content. As Sen. Frederick Frelinghuysen of New Jersey summarized the change,

> The "privileges and immunities" secured by the original Constitution were only such as each State gave to its own citizens. Each was prohibited from discriminating in favor of its own citizens and against the citizens of other States. But the fourteenth amendment prohibits the State from abridging the privileges or immunities of the citizens of the United States, whether its own citizens or any others. It not merely requires equality of privileges, but it demands that the privileges and immunities of all citizens shall be absolutely unabridged, unimpaired.

The framers referred repeatedly to the definition of privileges and immunities given by Justice Bushrod Washington in an 1825 decision called *Corfield v. Coryell.*[15] There, Washington defined privileges and immunities as rights "which are, in their nature, fundamental; which belong, of right, to the citizens of all free governments." He noted that such rights were so numerous that they "would perhaps be more tedious than difficult to enumerate." But he listed some of them, including "the enjoyment of life and liberty, with the right to acquire and possess property of every kind, and pursue and obtain happiness and safety, subject, nevertheless, to such restraints as the government may justly prescribe for the general good of the whole."

Regardless of the outer boundaries, it is clear that the framers considered privileges or immunities to protect a very broad category of rights against abridgement by the states. Sen. John Sherman of Ohio, one of the amendment's principal architects, defined privileges or immunities as "innumerable as the sands of the sea," encompassing not only the Bill of Rights but the rights set forth in the Declaration of Independence and those protected at common law.[16] Specifically, as Bingham, the amendment's principal House author put it, they encompassed "the liberty . . . to work in an honest calling and contribute by your toil in some sort to yourself, to the support of your fellowmen, and to be secure in the enjoyment of the fruits of your toil."[17] Sen. William T. Hamilton of Maryland agreed that "[i]f there is a right that is natural and that belongs to me because I am a citizen," it is the right "to transact my own private business in my own way without the interference of government"—the right of every person "to carry on his own occupation, to secure the fruits from his own industry . . . as long as it is a legitimate exercise of this right and not vicious in itself, or against public policy, or against the natural rights of others."[18] Sen. Matthew Carpenter of Wisconsin agreed that the privileges or immunities clause "offers all the pursuits and avocations of life." As Carpenter prophetically warned, "Strike down that amendment, or, what would be the same thing, construe it in such a niggardly spirit as to mean no more than the old Constitution meant, and you strike down the rights of the colored people all over this country."[19] That is, of course, exactly what happened, to the enduring detriment not only of blacks but of all Americans.

One can easily understand the excitement with which the Reconstruction Congress approved the Fourteenth Amendment. As Curtis recounts, "theirs was a transformed vision of federalism, with states required to respect the fundamental rights of American citizens."[20] The promise of the Declaration of Independence—that all individuals were possessed of inalienable rights that no government could abridge—finally would be fulfilled. Not just the federal government but the states would be bound at last to honor those rights.

But the excitement would be short-lived, for the Fourteenth Amendment's core protection was eviscerated before the ink was dry. As legal scholars Joseph Tussman and Jacobus tenBroek aptly observe, "the purposes of those framers received short shrift at the hands of the Supreme Court. . . . The privileges and immunities clause was officially killed in the *Slaughter-House cases*."[21]

As with so many landmark cases, the first to test the scope of the privileges or immunities clause emanated from an unusual source: in this case, a group of Louisiana butchers. In March 1869, the Louisiana Legislature enacted a statute granting an exclusive twenty-five-year slaughterhouse monopoly within New Orleans and other parishes, and ordering the closure of other slaughterhouses. The law also restricted the locations in which cattle could be landed and slaughtered, and established fees and an inspection process for such services.

As a lawyer who frequently has litigated "test" cases in various areas of the law, this factual scenario would ring alarm bells for me—especially in the historical setting of nineteenth-century Louisiana, in which predictably "deplorable sanitary conditions" surrounded the slaughtering of cattle.[22] If ever there was an industry in need of health and safety regulation, this would be it.

But, being Louisiana, that was not all there was to it. As historian Charles Lofgren recounts, "legislative bribery had greased passage of the law, with its most immediate beneficiaries—the seventeen participants in the corporation it established—adroitly distributing shares of stock and cash."[23] The monopoly had a devastating impact on many of the butchers who were not part of the deal.

Cacophony followed the law's passage. At one point more than two hundred suits were filed enforcing or attacking the law. Some of the challengers were bought off with land deals, shares of stock, or directorships in the monopoly. After a federal court order was issued to allow the butchers to ply their trade, supporters of the monopoly went to a newly created state court and procured an injunction against the butchers. New Orleans police, called out to enforce the injunction, confiscated all of the butchers' meat and allowed it to rot in the sun, leaving the city without meat for a weekend.[24]

Several cases circuitously made their way up to the U.S. Supreme Court and were consolidated as the *Slaughter-House Cases*. The principal argument made by the butchers was that the monopoly violated their privileges and immunities as citizens of the United States, recently guaranteed by the Fourteenth Amendment.

The question of whether the particular set of regulations was within the state's police power (that is, its power to regulate health and safety) presented a close question, but the applicability of the privileges or immunities clause to the question at hand should not have been in doubt. The court should have recognized that the rights guaranteed by the privileges or immunities clause protect all citizens against state governments, and that the grant of a slaughterhouse monopoly implicated rights protected by the clause. Had the court done so, the privileges or immunities clause would have survived even if the court ruled against the butchers on the grounds that the regulations were nonetheless justified by the state's police power. But the court was not content to construe the clause narrowly, or even to apply it in a manner deferential to the state's police power. Instead, it obliterated the clause and its precious protections.

It did so by a 5–4 margin—common today, but exceedingly rare in the 1870s. Today's court is divided along philosophical lines, but at that time it would have been difficult to predict the outcome of the *Slaughter-House Cases* based on the backgrounds, geographical origins, or political affiliations of the individual justices.[25] The justices in the majority voting to uphold the monopoly were a varied group. Justice Samuel F. Miller was a physician and lawyer, originally from Kentucky, who opposed slavery and joined the Whigs. He was appointed to the court by President Abraham Lincoln. Justice Nathan Clifford was a pro-slavery Democrat from Maine who served as attorney general under President James Knox Polk and was appointed to the court by President James Buchanan. Justice William Strong of Pennsylvania served as an abolitionist Democrat in the U.S. House of Representatives, and later became a Republican. He was appointed to the court by President Ulysses S. Grant. Strong was an accidental nominee, receiving the court nomination only after the initial nominee, Lincoln's Secretary of War Edwin Stanton, died before he could take his seat. All three served on the electoral commission that settled the presidential election of 1876—and though they agreed in the *Slaughter-House Cases*, they backed opposing candidates on the electoral commission, with Miller and Strong supporting Republican Rutherford B. Hayes and Clifford supporting Democrat Samuel Tilden.

The fourth member of the majority, Justice David Davis of Illinois, was Lincoln's campaign manager at the 1860 Republican presidential convention, and was appointed to the court by Lincoln. An independent, he would have been the swing vote on the 1876 electoral commission, but was elected to the U.S. Senate as a Democrat and gave up his seat on the commission.

Fittingly, the fifth vote in the *Slaughter-House Cases* was provided by one of the least-distinguished justices in the court's history, Ward Hunt. A lawyer and politician, Hunt was elected to various offices: first as a Democrat, then as a candidate of the Free Soil Party, and then as a Republican. Hunt, of New York, was an ally of political boss Roscoe Conkling, who persuaded Grant to appoint Hunt to the court. There he served for ten years without authoring a single majority opinion. His most famous judicial act was in 1872 when he ruled as a circuit judge that women's suffrage advocate Susan B. Anthony broke the law when she attempted to vote.

The dissenters likewise were diverse. Chief Justice Salmon Chase of Ohio, the only dissenter who did not author his own opinion, was a leading abolitionist who challenged Lincoln for the 1860 Republican presidential nomination, then served as Lincoln's secretary of the treasury until Lincoln nominated him to replace

Chief Justice Roger Taney in 1864. Perhaps equally distinguished was Justice Stephen Field, who served on the court for thirty-four years, from 1863 to 1897. Born in Connecticut, he moved to California and served as chief justice of the state supreme court. A pro-Union Democrat, he was appointed to the court by Lincoln to provide political and geographic balance. His pro-economic-liberty views in *Slaughter-House* and subsequent cases helped give rise after his death to the doctrine of substantive due process, discussed in the next section. Justice Joseph P. Bradley was a prominent commercial litigator from New Jersey who was appointed to the court by Grant. Bradley replaced Davis on the 1876 electoral commission and cast the deciding vote for Hayes. Justice Noah H. Swayne was an abolitionist lawyer who moved from his home state of Virginia to Ohio. He was Lincoln's first appointee and the first Republican ever to serve on the court.

Though seven of the justices were Republicans and only two (Clifford and Field) were Democrats, the decision did not break evenly on partisan lines. According to legal historians Ronald M. Labbe and Jonathan Lurie, who recently authored a book about the decision, Justice Clifford (the only justice appointed before the Civil War) had southern sympathies and "opposed expanded federal power." By contrast, Justice Field's decisions exhibited "a veneration for property rights and a hostility toward state regulation."[26] The Republicans reflected different beliefs as well.

The majority decision was written by Justice Miller. At the outset, Miller acknowledged the gravity of the task before the court, declaring that "[n]o questions so far-reaching and pervading in their consequences . . . have been before this court during the official life of any of its present members."[27] Yet, having recognized the momentous task of interpreting the new amendment for the first time, the majority promptly fumbled it badly.

Miller tipped his hand early on, arguing that the "one pervading purpose" of the Civil War constitutional amendments was to ensure "freedom of the slave race."[28] That was true of the Thirteenth Amendment, which abolished slavery; and it provided the principal motivation for creating the Fourteenth Amendment. But the privileges or immunities clause speaks in universal terms and protects all citizens. By suggesting that its pervading purpose focused on blacks, Miller set the stage for interpreting the clause narrowly (although he would construe it so narrowly that it would serve no purpose even for ensuring the freedom of blacks).

Then Miller got to the innovation that would consign the privileges or immunities clause to jurisprudential purgatory. Citing the amendment's protection of privileges or immunities of citizens of the United States, Miller divided the rights of citizenship into two classes. The first were the rights of national citizenship, which "owe their existence to the Federal government, its national character, its Constitution, or its laws." Those rights included the right of access to foreign commerce and to navigable waters, the right of habeas corpus, the right to move freely from one state to another and to enjoy the same rights as citizens of those states, and the right to assembly. The second was the broader category of civil rights generally, as enunciated by Justice Washington in *Corfield v. Coryell*, including the economic liberty asserted by the butchers.[29]

Prior to the Fourteenth Amendment, the first set of rights was protected by the U.S. Constitution; the second and broader category of rights was left to protection by the states only *if* the states chose to do so. Miller queried whether it was "the purpose of the fourteenth amendment, by the simple declaration that no State should make or enforce any law which shall abridge the privileges or immunities of *citizens of the United States*, to transfer the security and protection of all of the civil rights which we have mentioned, from the States to the Federal government?"[30]

The correct answer, to the extent that those rights were abridged by state governments, was obviously and emphatically yes. The whole point of the Fourteenth Amendment was that the states could not be trusted to reliably protect the fundamental rights of their own citizens. Not only slavery but the black codes proved that point and demonstrated the necessity of federal protection as a backstop to state protection of those rights. The artificial distinction between national and state citizenship and the notion that state citizenship was primary were abolished by the Fourteenth Amendment. As Rep. Frelinghuysen remarked, "The fourteenth amendment goes much further than the old Constitution. It makes United States citizenship primary, and state citizenship derivative."[31] In that way, as the U.S. Supreme Court recently described it, the Fourteenth Amendment "fundamentally altered our country's federal system."[32]

But the *Slaughter-House* majority didn't see things that way. Applying the clause to protect citizens from abuses of civil rights by their own states, Miller complained, "would constitute this court a perpetual censor upon all legislation of the States."[33] That was, of course, the point of the amendment. Yet the only limitation the Fourteenth Amendment placed upon the states, according to the majority, is that they must protect for their own citizens the handful of rights deriving from national citizenship—access to navigable waters, habeas corpus, and the like. The rest of the rights that the majority acknowledged were within the definition of "privileges or immunities"—including the economic liberty asserted by the butchers—continued to be among those "which belong to citizens of the States as such, and . . . [are not] placed under the special care of the Federal government."[34] For protection of those rights, citizens would continue to have to look to the states—which is to say that, despite the Fourteenth Amendment, they would have no meaningful recourse for violations of those rights by the states themselves.

In reaching its decision, the *Slaughter-House* majority did not look to the precipitating motivation behind the Fourteenth Amendment— the violation of civil rights by state governments—nor to clear legislative intent on key questions. Yet despite failing to do so, the majority gave the clause an extremely narrow construction, depriving it of even the meaning they ascribed to it. Ironically, as historians Labbe and Lurie note, "this interpretation of the privileges and immunities clause would later deprive the freedmen of any of its protections—in spite of Miller's earlier insistence that a concern for their freedom had pervaded all of the Reconstruction amendments."[35]

Indeed, the clause as construed by the majority would have little meaning at all. As Professor Curtis observes, "the privileges or immunities clause was virtually read out of the Constitution."[36] Professor Edward Corwin remarks that "[u]nique among constitutional provisions, the privileges and immunities clause of the Fourteenth Amendment enjoys the distinction of having been rendered a 'practical nullity' by a single decision of the Supreme Court within five years after its ratification."[37]

Justice Miller's decision provoked three dissenting opinions that were passionate in their denunciation of the majority's shocking departure from the Fourteenth Amendment's text, history, and purpose, but moderate in their approach to the law. The dissenters were not wild-eyed radicals who believed that the states have no power to regulate public health and safety, but instead interpreted the amendment to require the court to balance the state's legitimate interests against the important rights protected by the amendment.

Because Chief Justice Chase was suffering from deteriorating health, the task of writing the principal dissenting opinion fell to Justice Field. As Labbe and Lurie recount, "if there was any sense of hesitation or tentativeness in Miller's opinion, the same cannot be said of Field's. Now in his tenth year on the Court, he had already fashioned a judicial activism based on both his Jacksonian heritage and his own economic conservatism."[38]

Field, whose views were joined by all of the dissenters, acknowledged that the state's police power "undoubtedly extends to all regulations affecting the health, good order, morals, peace and safety of society," and "when these are not in conflict with any constitutional prohibitions, or fundamental principles, they cannot be successfully assailed in a judicial tribunal." However, he explained, "under the pretence of prescribing a police regulation the State cannot be permitted to encroach upon any of the just rights of the citizen, which the Constitution intended to secure against abridgement."[39] The judiciary's

role, Field asserted, was to look behind the alleged police power rationale to see if it justified a violation of protected rights.

Analyzing the regulations, Field had no difficulty in concluding
that the cattle landing and inspection requirements were legitimate
exercises of the police power. Moreover, he acknowledged that grants
of monopolies were permissible for "franchises of a public character,"
such as roads, bridges, and so forth. But such a public franchise, Field
reasoned, "is a very different thing from a grant, with exclusive privileges, of a right to pursue one of the ordinary trades or callings of life,
which is a right appertaining solely to the individual."[40]

The right to be free from monopolies was well-established in common law, and it accompanied the British colonists when they came
to the New World. "All monopolies in any known trade or manufacture are an invasion of these privileges, for they encroach upon the
liberty of citizens to acquire property and pursue happiness," Field
declared.[41] The "main ground" of the common law rule against monopolies, Field observed, "was their interference with the liberty of
the subject to pursue for his maintenance and that of his family any
lawful trade or employment. This liberty is assumed to be the natural
right of every Englishman."[42]

The Louisiana law, Field remarked, "presents the naked case, un-
accompanied by any public considerations, where a right to pursue a
lawful and necessary calling, previously enjoyed by every citizen, and
in connection with which a thousand persons were daily employed,
is taken away and vested exclusively . . . in a single corporation."[43]

The issue before the court, Field stated, was "nothing less than the
question whether the recent Amendments to the Federal Constitution protect citizens of the United States against the deprivation of
their common rights by State legislation."[44] Looking at the purpose of
the Fourteenth Amendment, the answer clearly was yes, for it "was
adopted to obviate objections which had been raised and pressed with
great force to the validity of the Civil Rights Act, and to place the
common rights of the American citizens under the protection of the
National government."[45]

Those rights, Field explained, were not created by the Fourteenth Amendment, but were pre-existing rights whose protection now was guaranteed against abridgement by the states. "All monopolies in any known trade or manufacture are an invasion of these privileges," he stated, "for they encroach upon the liberty of citizens to acquire property and pursue happiness."[46] As Field declared, if the Fourteenth Amendment "has no reference to privileges and immunities of this character . . . it was a vain and idle enactment, which accomplished nothing, and most unnecessarily excited Congress and the people on its passage."[47] As for the challenged monopoly, Field lamented, "it is to me a matter of profound regret that its validity is recognized by a majority of this court, for by it the right of free labor, one of the most sacred and imprescriptible rights of man, is violated."[48]

In a separate dissenting opinion, Justice Bradley, joined by Justice Swayne, also began by acknowledging the police power of the states, articulating the appropriate line when it comes into conflict with fundamental rights: the state "may prescribe the manner of their exercise, but it cannot subvert the rights themselves."[49] He then set forth the two-part inquiry that the court should conduct. First, "[i]s it one of the rights and privileges of a citizen of the United States to pursue such civil employment as he may choose to adopt, subject to such reasonable regulations as may be prescribed by law?" If so, the court should determine whether the law is "a reasonable regulation of that employment which the legislature has a right to impose."[50]

Tracing economic liberty to common law, the Declaration of Independence, and *Corfield v. Coryell*, Justice Bradley found that the first part of the inquiry was satisfied:

> For the preservation, exercise, and enjoyment of [his] rights the individual citizen, as a necessity, must be free to adopt such calling, profession, or trade as may seem to him most conducive. . . . Without this right he cannot be a freeman. This right to choose one's calling is an essential part of that liberty which it is the object of government to protect; and a calling, when chosen, is a man's property and right.

Liberty and property are not protected where these rights are arbitrarily assailed.[51]

Having found that the law implicated a fundamental right, Bradley turned to the second inquiry: whether the restriction was a valid part of the police power. The statute's prescription of locations for slaughterhouses and its inspection standards, he found, were "clearly a police regulation." But "[t]o compel a butcher . . . to slaughter [his] cattle in another person's slaughter-house and pay him a toll therefor," Bradley concluded, "is such a restriction upon the trade as materially to interfere with its prosecution." Such a monopoly, he declared, is invalid as "one of those arbitrary and unjust laws made in the interest of a few scheming individuals."[52]

Swayne dissented separately as well, placing the Fourteenth Amendment in its historical context and assailing the majority for subverting the clear intent of the amendment's framers. "By the Constitution, as it stood before the war," Swayne recounted, "ample protection was given against oppression by the Union, but little was given against wrong and oppression by the States. That want was intended to be supplied by this amendment."[53] The first eleven amendments to the Constitution "were intended to be checks and limitations" upon the national government, he observed.[54] But "the light of experience" revealed to the public that "there was less danger of tyranny in the head than of anarchy and tyranny in the members."[55]

As a consequence, Swayne explained, Congress adopted the Civil War amendments, which "are a new departure, and mark an important epoch in the constitutional history of the country," for they "trench directly upon the power of the States, and deeply affect those bodies." Thus understood, Swayne declared, "these amendments may be said to rise to the dignity of a new Magna Charta."[56] Swayne lamented that the majority opinion "defeats, by a limitation not anticipated, the intent of those by whom the instrument was framed."[57]

It is an apt description of the *Slaughter-House Cases* that they took a provision intended to be a new Magna Carta and turned it into a constitutional nullity. The majority justifiably could have upheld the monopoly as an exercise of the police power in the special case of a hazardous activity without gutting the privileges or immunities clause. But instead it went much further, essentially repealing the provision by judicial fiat.

The decision is a clarion example that the worst excesses of judicial power occur not through activism but through abdication.[58] Judicial activism lies in the eye of the beholder, and often means nothing more than a decision with which someone disagrees. The simplest and most objective definition of judicial activism is when courts invoke constitutional guarantees to strike down laws. So defined, I believe the main problem with judicial activism is not that there is too much of it, but not nearly enough. Some advocates of "judicial restraint," such as Professor Robert Bork, believe that judicial review of government decisions should be limited or nonexistent. Not surprisingly, Bork views the *Slaughter-House Cases* as "a narrow victory for judicial moderation.[59] Bork says that a "provision whose meaning cannot be ascertained is precisely like a provision that is written in Sanskrit or is obliterated past deciphering by an ink blot. No judge is entitled to interpret an ink blot on the ground that there must be something under it."[60]

With respect to Bork, the privileges or immunities clause is not an ink blot, nor was it written in Sanskrit. It had a clearly established meaning when it was written—a meaning that is obscure today only because the Supreme Court removed the term from the legal lexicon. It seems to me there is nothing a court can do that is more damaging to the rule of law than draining a constitutional provision of meaning and leaving its intended beneficiaries defenseless against government oppression. That is not judicial moderation, it is judicial lawlessness.

Most legal scholars on both the left and the right disdain the *Slaughter-House Cases.* As Harvard Law Professor Laurence Tribe put it, "there is considerable consensus among constitutional thinkers that the Supreme Court made a scandalously wrong decision in this case."

The late Yale Law Professor Charles Black described the opinion as "probably the worst holding, in its effect on human rights, ever uttered by the Supreme Court."[61] But the decision stands today, more than 135 years later, an enduring black mark on American jurisprudence.

Despite the court majority's decision to eviscerate the core provision of the Fourteenth Amendment, Swayne expressed in his dissenting opinion the "hope that the consequences to follow may prove less serious and far-reaching than the minority fear they will be."[62] But in fact, the consequences of the *Slaughter-House Cases* have been disastrous, in ways that even the dissenters likely could not have contemplated. As the next section will describe in further detail, at least four major adverse consequences can be attributed to the *Slaughter-House Cases*:

1. First and foremost, the major constitutional protection for economic liberty was obliterated. When the U.S. Supreme Court eventually decided to revive judicial protection for economic liberty, because the privileges or immunities clause was no longer viable, it felt compelled to do so under the due process clause, which was not a logical fit. When a New Deal court more hostile to economic liberty emerged, it was able to make quick work of the doctrine. Today, judges of every philosophical stripe believe that the court's venture into protection of economic liberty was a misadventure. As a result, economic liberty is relegated to the status of a constitutional orphan, unloved and unsheltered.

2. In immediate terms, the *Slaughter-House Cases* permitted the economic subjugation of blacks, leading directly to *Plessy v. Ferguson*,[63] which sanctioned the dreaded Jim Crow laws. By depriving those who challenged laws decreeing "separate but equal" accommodations of their strongest legal argument—freedom of contract—*Slaughter-House* forced them to use their second-best argument, equal protection. Though the concept of equal protection, rooted in concerns about special-interest legislation, should have prevented the

Jim Crow laws, it was difficult to argue against racial segregation when the framers largely believed the amendment did not outlaw it. Had *Slaughter-House* been decided differently, it is likely that the discriminatory streetcar laws would have been invalidated as a violation of economic liberty under the privileges or immunities clause, thereby allowing countless generations of black and other minority Americans to earn a share of the American Dream and sparing our nation more than a century of tumult. Instead, the civil rights movement increasingly focused on equality rather than economic empowerment, a philosophical and strategic shift that has had long-lasting and not entirely positive ramifications.[64]

3. As Curtis aptly observes, the court's narrow construction of the Fourteenth Amendment "effectively nullified the intent to apply the Bill of Rights to the states."[65] As with economic liberty, the court eventually would get around to applying the Bill of Rights to the states, but only some of those rights—in essence, protecting only the rights that the justices preferred and not others (such as, until recently, the right to keep and bear arms under the Second Amendment). The muddled and discredited "selective incorporation" doctrine is on its last legs. But still, the court has declined to remove the application of the Bill of Rights from its shaky jurisprudential moorings in the due process clause and give it the firmer ground it deserves—in the privileges or immunities clause.

4. Finally, by opening the door for the court to create a vessel in the due process clause for all rights it might want to protect, the *Slaughter-House Cases* created all manner of judicial mischief. Were the court to have recognized the privileges or immunities clause as the sole source of substantive rights under the Fourteenth Amendment, it would have created a conceptual construct by which to identify those rights— specifically, rights that existed at common law or that were

recognized by the Declaration of Independence, the Constitution, and the Civil Rights Act of 1866. Instead, the murky doctrine of "substantive due process" contains no such limiting principles. Among the rights recognized under the due process clause is abortion, which would have been very difficult to have found in the definition of privileges or immunities. Ironically, conservatives like Bork who have commended *Slaughter-House* as an exercise in judicial restraint have overlooked the perverse jurisprudential by-product it spawned.

That is a lot to lay at the doorstep of a single judicial opinion. But it is all the foreseeable consequence of a decision that nullified one of our Constitution's most important provisions, preventing it from achieving its twin goals, as described by Justice Thomas, of protecting against "the willfulness of both run-amok majorities and run-amok judges."[66] In the next section I will sketch in greater detail the pernicious legacy of the *Slaughter-House Cases*, and then turn my attention to the hopeful developments that may lead to its long-overdue demise.

PART 3

THE AFTERMATH OF SLAUGHTER-HOUSE

O NE MIGHT THINK that after such a tragic and lawless decision by the nation's highest court, prospects were about
as bleak as they could be in terms of protection of economic liberty
and, more generally, of the basic civil rights of citizens against oppressive state governments. But in fact, glimmers of hope appeared even
on the face of the *Slaughter-House Cases*.

First and foremost, all nine members of the Supreme Court agreed
that economic liberty is a fundamental right, one of the privileges or
immunities of citizens. They disagreed over the important question of
whether that right was protected against abridgement by the states
under the Fourteenth Amendment; but they did not disagree that it
is a fundamental right. The promise of that powerful consensus was
thwarted by *Slaughter-House*; but so long as the consensus remained,
it could be vindicated when the composition of the court changed.

Second, the court expressly left open the question of what rights
pertained to individuals by virtue of national citizenship.[1] As legal
historians Labbe and Lurie observe, Justice Miller "may not have intended his opinion to be taken as an 'all embracing construction' of the
Fourteenth Amendment."[2] By describing privileges or immunities as
those that "owe their existence to the Federal government, its national

character, its Constitution, or its laws," the *Slaughter-House* majority left the door open to recognition of additional rights that might be protected against abridgement by the states. For instance, the court curiously mentioned freedom of assembly, which is protected by the First Amendment. That might imply that the entire Bill of Rights would be applied to the states—an outcome entirely consistent with the framers' intent that would dramatically increase the protection of citizens against state government tyranny.

But over time, both of those hopes would be snuffed out. Economic liberty enjoyed a temporary revival, but then was consigned to bottom-tier status as one of the least-important, least-protected rights.[3] And, at least until the present day, the privileges or immunities of citizens have not been protected beyond the narrow list contained in *Slaughter-House*—not even to protect freedom of assembly, much less the remainder of the Bill of Rights. Even worse, the judicial abdication initiated in the *Slaughter-House Cases* would infect other protections of the Fourteenth Amendment as well.

All of which is to say that this section of the book makes for depressing reading. Good thing there is one more section after this.

Not surprisingly, the *Slaughter-House* decision was roundly condemned for having defeated the promise and purpose of the Fourteenth Amendment. Referring to the earlier *Dred Scott* ruling that had determined that blacks had no rights under the law, Sen. Timothy Howe of Wisconsin declared that his view of the *Slaughter-House Cases* was the same as what "the civilized world have already said of another . . . decision of that same court, that it is not law and cannot be law."[4] Political scientist John W. Burgess charged that *Slaughter-House* repudiated the "great gain in the domain of civil liberty won by the terrible exertion of the nation by appeal to arms. I have perfect confidence that the day will come when it will be seen to be intensely reactionary and will be overruled."[5] But that day, of course, has not yet arrived.

Likewise, Congress lacked the political will to try to overrule the decision. During the five years between the ratification of the Fourteenth Amendment and the *Slaughter-House Cases*, fervor for protecting the rights of the freedmen waned. Despite President Grant's passion for protecting the freedmen, his administration's scandals provided a major distraction. Aging radical Republicans were replaced by newcomers with greater sympathy toward states' rights, especially in 1874 when Democrats recaptured control of Congress. The increasing need for military force to ensure the rights of blacks sapped the political capital of some of their greatest political allies. The rise of the Ku Klux Klan raised political stakes even further. Reconciliation replaced reconstruction as the primary national goal, culminating with the 1876 presidential election contest between Rutherford Hayes and Samuel Tilden, which was fought to a draw that was resolved in the Republican's favor only on the condition that Reconstruction would be phased out.[6]

Meanwhile, the Supreme Court made quick work of extinguishing any prospect that something might be salvaged from the privileges or immunities clause following the *Slaughter-House Cases*. In *Bradwell v. State*, decided just after *Slaughter-House*, Myra Bradwell challenged her exclusion from the Illinois bar as a violation of the privileges or immunities of citizens under the Fourteenth Amendment. Bradwell passed the bar examination and was found to possess all of the requisite qualifications, save one: as a married woman, under state law she lacked capacity to sign binding contracts, and therefore she was found ineligible to practice law.

Though the question of whether butchers had enforceable rights under the privileges or immunities clause closely divided the court, in this case only Chief Justice Chase dissented from the decision denying Bradwell's admission to the practice of law (and he did so without an opinion). "The opinion just delivered in the *Slaughter-House Cases* renders elaborate argument in the present case unnecessary," remarked Justice Miller in his opinion for the majority, "for, unless we are wholly and radically mistaken in the principles on which those cases are decided, the right to control and regulate the granting of license to practice law in the courts of a State is one of those powers which are not transferred for its protection to the Federal government."[7] Not only blacks and butchers, but now women, were precluded from looking to the federal courts for recourse against subjugation by their state governments.

One might have expected Justices Bradley, Field, and Swayne to leap to Bradwell's defense, invoking the transcendent principles they championed in their dissenting opinions in *Slaughter-House*, but that would be placing too much stock in the enlightenment of the age in which they served on the court. Bradwell's claim, explained Bradley, "is based upon the supposed right of every person, man or woman, to engage in any lawful employment for a livelihood"[8]—a right Bradley seemed to defend pretty forcefully in his *Slaughter-House* dissent. But the rub for Bradley was "man *or woman*." For "the civil law, as well as nature herself," declared Bradley, "has always recognized a wide difference in the respective destinies of man and woman." He went on to assert, "Man is, or should be, woman's protector and defender. The natural and proper timidity and delicacy which belongs to the female sex evidently unfits it for many of the occupations of civil life," including the law. The "paramount destiny and mission of woman," he asserted, "are to fulfill the noble and benign offices of wife and mother."[9] Thus did Bradley and two of his fellow justices, who so boldly and expansively had proclaimed the privileges or immunities of citizenship in *Slaughter-House*, at the very same time demonstrated that they could be every bit as hypocritical as the members of the court they had assailed in that decision, in this instance by draining the term citizenship of meaning for half the nation's population.

Prospects for protecting freedom under the Fourteenth Amendment suffered further grievous harm shortly thereafter in *U.S. v. Cruikshank*. Ironically, the facts traced back to the year that *Slaughter-House* was decided. In an 1873 incident known as the Colfax Massacre, a group of armed white men brutally murdered as many as 165 mainly unarmed black men. Among the white assailants, ninety-seven were indicted, but only nine went to trial, and six of those were acquitted of all charges. The remaining three were acquitted of murder but convicted under the federal Enforcement Act of 1870 for banding together and depriving their victims of constitutional rights, including freedom of assembly under the First Amendment and the Second Amendment right to keep and bear arms.[10]

The Court decided, over a single dissent, that the Fourteenth Amendment did not protect the rights set forth in the Second Amendment, thus extinguishing the hope that *Slaughter-House* would allow protection of the Bill of Rights against the states under the privileges or immunities clause. The Enforcement Act was designed especially to enforce the rights of newly emancipated blacks, thus falling squarely within the core purpose of the Fourteenth Amendment identified by the *Slaughter-House* majority. The law made it a felony for people to band together and conspire to deprive any person "of any right or privilege granted or secured to him by the constitution or the laws of the United States."

The court's reasoning was truly astounding:

> The right of the people peaceably to assemble for lawful purposes existed long before the adoption of the Constitution of the United States. . . . It "derives its source . . . from those laws whose authority is acknowledged by civilized man throughout the world." It is found wherever civilization exists. It was not, therefore, a right granted to the people by the Constitution. . . . As no direct power over it was granted to Congress, it remains . . . subject to State jurisdiction.[11]

By this logic, the purpose of the privileges or immunities clause was completely repudiated. Even in *Slaughter-House*, all of the justices recognized that privileges or immunities were precisely those rights that existed as a matter of course in free governments, dating back to the common law that preexisted the Constitution. Moreover, the rights at issue in *Cruikshank* were expressly protected by the Bill of Rights. Indeed, the *Slaughter-House* majority acknowledged that freedom of assembly, in particular, was one of the rights that owed its existence to federal citizenship.

But here the court grounded its decision in the notion that any right that preexisted the Constitution could not be a right granted by the Constitution. Technically, that may be correct, in that the Constitution did not grant rights, but rather granted the federal government limited powers. The Constitution did, however—as the Ninth Amendment in its protection of un-enumerated rights makes clear—preserve and protect rights that preexisted the Constitution. Under this reading, the privileges or immunities clause protects virtually *nothing*, because most if not all of the rights protected by the Constitution can be said to have preexisted the Constitution. Moreover, under *Cruikshank*, the rights preexisting the Constitution were left—as they had been prior to the Fourteenth Amendment—entirely to the states to protect, even though it was the states' failure to protect those rights that principally animated the adoption of the Fourteenth Amendment. All of which meant that the states were unleashed to violate those rights with no constraint, calling into serious question exactly which side had won the Civil War. And yet, as radically as the court departed from the framers' intent, *Cruikshank* remains largely intact in stating the law applicable to the privileges or immunities clause 135 years later.

Not surprisingly, state governments and their apologists took advantage of the state of constitutional anarchy created by *Slaughter-House* and its progeny. Congressional Democrats successfully argued for the removal of school desegregation provisions from the Civil Rights Act of 1875, on the grounds that Congress had no remedial authority under the Fourteenth Amendment beyond protecting the narrow range of rights owing their existence to national citizenship.[12] Southern states replaced the black codes with Jim Crow laws, decreeing segregation and limiting economic opportunities for blacks, especially through ostensibly race-neutral laws regulating labor contracts and restricting entry into trades and professions.[13] At the same time, legal advocates challenging such laws largely abandoned the privileges or immunities clause following *Cruikshank*. Instead, "[r]elying instead on the less substantive Due Process Clause . . . and then on the still less substantive Equal Protection Clause," as Kimberly C. Shankman and Roger Pilon observe, "courts have fashioned a Fourteenth Amendment jurisprudence that would be all but unrecognizable to those who wrote the amendment."[14]

Private businesses and colleges chafed under the separate-but-equal laws, and they looked for ways to challenge them. On its face, the Fourteenth Amendment's guarantee of equal protection ought to have precluded blatantly unequal state legislation. Its general and universal terms unquestionably embraced the principles expressed by James Madison in *The Federalist No. 10*, warning that factions would manipulate democratic processes to redistribute opportunities to their advantage unless constrained by a robust concept of equality. Indeed, Sen. Jacob Howard of Michigan declared that the intent of Congress in enacting the Fourteenth Amendment was to "abolish all caste legislation and do away with the injustice of subjecting one caste of persons to a code not applicable to another."[15] Likewise, Sen. Thaddeus Stevens proclaimed that henceforth, "no distinction would be tolerated in this purified Republic but what arose from merit or conduct."[16]

Those like me who believe in interpreting the Constitution through "textualism"—that is, applying the clear text of the Constitution and resorting to an inquiry into intent only where the text is not clear—would have no difficulty finding that the equal protection guarantee forbids separate-but-equal laws. But segregation was a widespread practice at the time the Fourteenth Amendment was adopted—not just in the South but in the North. By contrast with the privileges or immunities clause, which everyone agreed was inspired by the desire to eradicate the black codes, it was a much taller order to argue that the equal protection clause was intended to eradicate segregation. But *Slaughter-House* removed the privileges or immunities clause from the litigation arsenal of those who wanted to protect equal opportunity, leaving them no option but to resort to the equal protection clause—as it turned out, to disastrous effect.

The case of *Plessy v. Ferguson* was part of a legal strategy supported by the Louisiana and Nashville Railroad, which wanted to topple state laws that forced railroads to separate service between white and colored cars.[17] Homer Adolph Plessy was enlisted as a plaintiff in a test case because he was light-skinned and only one-eighth black—enough to qualify for colored-car status under Louisiana's law.[18]

By an 8–1 vote, the court in 1896 affirmed the Louisiana law in one of its most infamous decisions. Writing for the majority, Justice Henry B. Brown acknowledged that the object of the equal protection clause "was undoubtedly to enforce the absolute equality of the two races before the law." Indeed. However, Brown went on, "in the nature of things, it could not have been intended to abolish distinctions based upon color, or to enforce social, as distinguished from political equality, or a commingling of the two races upon terms unsatisfactory to either." Laws requiring separation of the races "do not necessarily imply the inferiority of either race to the other," Brown explained, "and have been generally, if not universally, recognized as within the competency of the state legislatures in the exercise of their police power."[19]

Justice John M. Harlan was the sole dissenter, decrying a statute that was plainly "inconsistent with the personal liberty of citizens, white and black."[20] Harlan's passionate dissent was a clarion call to vindicate the principles of equality espoused by the Constitution's framers, yet so long denied. "There is no caste here," Harlan proclaimed. "Our Constitution is color-blind, and neither knows nor tolerates classes among citizens. In respect of civil rights, all citizens are equal before the law."[21]

The legacy of *Slaughter-House* and *Plessy*—the twin pillars of judicial abdication in enforcing the Fourteenth Amendment—lived on together for a long time. Only eight years after *Plessy*, the court sustained a fine by the state of Kentucky against a private post-secondary institution, Berea College, for admitting blacks as a proper exercise of the state's authority over corporations. Harlan again dissented, charging to no avail that "the statute is an arbitrary invasion of the rights of liberty and property guaranteed by the Fourteenth Amendment against hostile state action, and is, therefore, void."[22] Harlan was absolutely correct, of course, but his argument was foreclosed by the precedential impact of *Slaughter-House* and *Plessy*. As a result, states were free to run roughshod over the civil rights of all Americans, especially blacks.

But defenders of economic liberty had not given up. Even in *Slaughter-House*, the members of the court all had agreed that economic liberty was a fundamental civil right—a consensus that, sadly, no longer exists today. They disagreed on the critical question of whether it was a right attributable to national or state citizenship. In *Slaughter-House*, the latter view prevailed, thus removing protection for economic liberty under the U.S. Constitution. But the widespread belief in the importance of economic liberty in the pantheon of civil rights led to a brief period during which it gained judicial protection against state abrogation under the Fourteenth Amendment in the late nineteenth and early twentieth centuries, albeit under the due process protection rather than the privileges or immunities clause.[23]

Undeterred by his defeat in *Slaughter-House*, Justice Field began laying the intellectual groundwork for protecting economic liberty under the due process clause only three years after that decision. In *Munn v. Illinois*, owners of grain silos brought suit against a state law that limited the prices they could charge for storing grain. The law was brought about by farmers, who had greater political clout in the state legislature than the silo owners. Under prior decisions, states could regulate only common carriers, businesses that caused nuisances, and natural monopolies, but in *Munn* the Court expanded state regulatory authority, upholding the statute because the regulated businesses were "affected with a public interest."[24]

Field dissented from the court's recognition of such sweeping and open-ended regulatory power. Arguing that the "receipt and storage of grain in a building erected by private means . . . does not constitute the building of a public warehouse," Field stated that the court's ruling meant that "all property and all business in the State" henceforth would be "held at the mercy of a majority of its legislature."[25]

Though Field lost that battle, his argument that economic regulations could not permissibly displace consensual and non-harmful private contractual arrangements was an early expression of the doctrine of "substantive due process"—the notion that excessive or unjustified restrictions on property or liberty could violate the guarantee of due process. It may have been for Field a case of the ends justifying the means—the framers of the Fourteenth Amendment meant to protect economic liberty, and he would vindicate that purpose one way or the other. But though the underlying principle was sound, its grounding not in the privileges or immunities clause but in the due process clause means that the right is bounded neither by constitutional text nor intent but by judges' views of what is encompassed within "liberty" and "property." Though economic liberty has long ceased to enjoy significant protection under the due process clause, more recent courts, for instance, have found abortion to be encompassed within the definition of liberty, and welfare checks and government employment encompassed within the meaning of property.

Still, the idea of substantive due process grew; by the close of the nineteenth century, a majority of the Supreme Court agreed that the protection of liberty under the due process clause included the individual's right "to earn his livelihood by any lawful calling; to pursue any livelihood or avocation; and for that purpose to enter into all contracts which may be proper, necessary, and essential" to earning a livelihood.[26]

Although the due process clause was the star of the era, the equal protection clause made some guest appearances. Conceptually, wielding equal protection in such contexts often made more sense than substantive due process, because many of the challenged economic regulations (as in *Munn*) were procured by interests seeking to reallocate benefits and burdens for their advantage—classic "faction" legislation that is in constant tension with the guarantee of equality under law.

Most noteworthy in this regard is one of the few economic liberty decisions from this period to survive as healthy precedent in our time, *Yick Wo v. Hopkins*. The court struck down a San Francisco ordinance that limited laundries to those constructed of brick or stone, a thinly disguised attempt to drive Chinese entrepreneurs, whose laundries were constructed of wood, out of business. The court found the dividing line to be subject to invidious manipulation by the board of supervisors, holding that "the very idea that one man may be compelled to hold his life, or the means of living, or any material right essential to the enjoyment of life, at the mere will of another, seems to be intolerable in any country where freedom prevails, as being the essence of slavery itself."[27]

The renaissance of economic liberty experienced its apotheosis in a 1905 case, *Lochner v. New York*. The state enacted the Bakeshop Act, which established health and safety standards for bakeries, but also limited employment in bakeries to ten hours per day and sixty hours per week. As a consequence, the law established a de facto ceiling for what bakery workers could earn. Bakery owner Joseph Lochner violated the law and was convicted.[28]

The Supreme Court overturned the conviction. The majority ruled that the state's police power must be weighed against liberty of contract. "Otherwise the Fourteenth Amendment would have no efficacy and the legislatures of the States would have unbounded power," the court declared.[29] "Both property and liberty are held on such reasonable conditions as may be imposed" by the state in exercising its police powers, the court acknowledged, "and with such conditions the Fourteenth Amendment was not designed to interfere."[30] But the court sagely remarked that "many of the laws of this character, while passed under what is claimed to be the police power for the purpose of protecting the public health or welfare, are, in reality, passed from other motives."[31] If the judiciary failed to safeguard the individual against such abuses, the majority reasoned, "[n]o trade, no occupation, no mode of earning one's living, could escape this all-pervading power . . . although such limitation might seriously cripple the ability of the laborer to support himself and his family."[32] That is, of course, an apt description of where we find ourselves more than a century after those words were written.

Under the rule of law applied by the majority, regulations designed to protect health or safety were permissible. But there was "no reasonable ground for interfering with the liberty of the person or the right of free contract, by determining the hours of labor, in the occupation of a baker."[33] The state made no showing that the number of hours was connected either to the health of employees or the quality of the bread. Thus, the law was "an unreasonable, unnecessary, and arbitrary interference with the right of the individual to his personal liberty or to enter into those contracts in relation to labor which may seem to him appropriate or necessary for the support of himself and his family."[34]

The majority decision in *Lochner* is a celebration of freedom of enterprise and freedom of contract, and a repudiation of government paternalism and excessive regulation. It reflects a careful and proper balancing of freedom and the state's police power. It would not prevent the state from enacting valid public health or safety laws, regulating such matters as child labor or coercion in the workplace, or protecting against consumer fraud. But it did prevent the state from arbitrarily limiting opportunities and the autonomy of individuals to make economic decisions in their own best interest. It achieved, through the due process clause, the goals the Fourteenth Amendment's framers intended to protect through the privileges or immunities clause. But by invoking the due process clause, it placed the protection of economic liberty on intellectually shaky footing.

Justice Harlan authored a dissenting opinion for three justices. They agreed with the important principle that the state "may not unduly interfere with the right of the citizen to enter into contracts that may be necessary and essential in the enjoyment of the inherent rights belonging to every one," among which is the right "to earn his livelihood by any lawful calling, to pursue any livelihood or avocation."[35] But unlike the majority, the dissenters concluded that "this statute was enacted in order to protect the physical well-being of those who work in [a] bakery" and therefore was a permissible exercise of the police power.[36] Significantly, the main dissenters did not disagree with the majority that economic liberty is an "inherent" right or that the Fourteenth Amendment protects that right against "undue" interference by the state. Even had the court's ruling gone the other way, if this common ground prevailed as the rule of law, our nation would enjoy far greater economic liberty than it does today.

The seeds of the demise of judicial protection for economic liberty were planted in a separate dissenting opinion by Justice Oliver Wendell Holmes, one of the most statist justices ever to sit on the Supreme Court. Though it was joined by no other justice, the Holmes dissent established the rationale for *carte blanche* economic regulation that would prevail a few decades later and for the following seventy-five years and counting.

"This case is decided upon an economic theory which a large part of the country does not entertain," Holmes proclaimed, namely, the "shibboleth" of the "liberty of the citizen to do as he likes so long as he does not interfere with the liberty of others to do the same."[37] A constitution, Holmes asserted, "is not intended to embody a particular economic theory, whether of paternalism and the organic relation of the citizen to the State or of laissez faire. It is made for people of fundamentally differing views."[38]

It is true that the Constitution tolerates—indeed, protects—people with fundamentally differing views, and it allows a broad diversity of public policy. But it also establishes the basic rule of law within which such policies must accord themselves, and that rule of law reflects the principles of the founders, which place great value on liberty and property. For Holmes, not only did views on economic policy change over time, but constitutional rules evolved to accommodate them. And of course, each succeeding generation, from the New Deal to the Great Society to the current one, has witnessed evergreater government interference with economic liberty. Holmes is the godfather of the contemporary anything-goes judicial approach to economic regulation.

Yet even Holmes's dissenting opinion contains the limiting principle that he and subsequent judges should have applied. The "word 'liberty,' in the 14th Amendment, is perverted when it is held to prevent the natural outcome of a dominant opinion," Holmes declared, sounding more than a little like Robert Bork. But then comes the caveat: "unless it can be said that a rational and fair man necessarily would admit that the statute proposed would infringe fundamental principles as they have been understood by the traditions of our people and our law."

That is an exact description of the privileges or immunities of citizens, which encompass freedom of enterprise. Contrary to Holmes's assertions, freedom of enterprise was not a passing economic fad embraced for the moment by the majority of the Supreme Court. It was a core value of the framers of the Fourteenth Amendment, who in turn traced it to the Declaration of Independence, which in turn was rooted in the common law. The rights embraced by the Fourteenth Amendment were intended to be subject to the proper exercise of the state's police power, but not to the passing whims or oppressions of "dominant opinion." Like all of the rights protected by our Constitution, the Fourteenth Amendment's trilogy of protections was intended to be asserted by the individual or the minority against the majority and the outcomes of democratic processes when manipulated by special-interest groups. Indeed, the Fourteenth Amendment is so perceived by the Supreme Court today—except when it comes to rights, such as economic liberty, that are relegated to "rational basis" review. For those rights, which today exist only in theory and memory but not in fact, we have Holmes to thank for four generations of judicial abdication.

The clash between economic liberty and government regulation came into sharp focus in the early years of the New Deal. As would later be the case during the early years of the Obama administration, the executive and legislative branches of the federal government were dominated by liberal Democrats while the U.S. Supreme Court had a tenuous 5–4 majority that was determined to protect individual rights. The court invalidated a number of New Deal enactments, caus-ing the administration considerable annoyance. In 1937, President Franklin D. Roosevelt threatened to expand the size of the court, thus allowing him to pack it with justices who were more tolerant of ex-panded government power. The pressure was tremendous, leading the swing justice, Owen Roberts, to align with the New Deal, which be-came known as "the switch in time that saved nine." In the process, however, the court abandoned the protection of economic liberty that it had championed for the better part of four decades.

The erosion began in earnest in 1933 with the court's decision in *Nebbia v. New York*. The case involved a New York statute that em-powered the Milk Control Board to set minimum prices for milk—an overtly protectionist regulation that added to the misery of families during the Depression—and to make it a crime to sell milk below that price. The Legislature justified the law on the basis that the milk industry was related to "the well being of our citizens" and "the strength and vigor of the race," which therefore served the pub-lic interest. Leo Nebbia was convicted for violating the minimum price law by selling milk below the prescribed prices.[39]

The court upheld the conviction, holding that "a state is free to adopt whatever economic policy may reasonably be deemed to pro-mote public welfare," provided that "the laws passed are seen to have a reasonable relation to a proper legislative purpose, and are neither arbitrary nor discriminatory."[40] It may seem shocking—particularly in a nation whose moral claim is staked in its doctrinal commitment to opportunity—that a person could be convicted of a crime for sell-ing milk below a prescribed price. Yet that was the perverse conse-quence of the abandonment of meaningful judicial review of economic regulations.

Just how deferential the new "rational basis" standard would be was illustrated three years later in *West Coast Hotel Co. v. Parrish*. By a 5–4 vote, the court upheld a Washington state law establishing a mini-mum wage for women and children, overturning a prior decision[41] that had applied *Lochner* to strike down a similar law. Instead of weighing the necessity of the regulation against its burden on economic liberty, the court presumed its constitutionality, smugly (and incorrectly) asserting that the "Constitution does not speak of freedom of contract."[42] Borrowing from the patronizing stereotypes expressed by Justice Joseph Bradley a half-century earlier, Chief Justice Charles Evans Hughes emphasized that the contracting parties were women, "in whose protection the State has a special interest" justified by the "woman's physical structure and the performance of maternal functions"[43] and by their "unequal position with respect to bargaining power" that renders them "defenceless against the denial of a living wage."[44] Allowing employers to freely contract for wages below the minimum decreed by the state, Hughes declared, would amount to "a subsidy for unconscionable employers. The community may direct its law-making power to correct the abuse which springs from their selfish disregard of the public interest."[45]

Justice George Sutherland issued an eloquent dissent. "It is urged that the question involved should now receive fresh consideration . . . because of 'the economic conditions which have supervened'," he remarked, "but the meaning of the Constitution does not change with the ebb and flow of economic events."[46] Taking a more realistic and enlightened view than Hughes, Sutherland insisted that the "ability to make a fair bargain . . . does not depend upon [a person's] sex."[47] The rule discarded by the majority had never been that freedom of contract was absolute, Sutherland observed, but that "freedom of contract was the general rule and restraint the exception; and that the power to abridge that freedom could only be justified by the existence of exceptional circumstances."[48] By adopting the rational basis test, the Court reversed that rule: regulations restricting freedom of contract would be sustained except under exceptional circumstances.

Perhaps recognizing that they were fighting a losing battle over substantive due process, the conservative justices made a brief foray at reviving the privileges or immunities clause. In *Colgate v. Harvey*, the court considered a discriminatory tax scheme imposed by Vermont. The court noted the anomaly that the right to conduct a lawful business outside of a person's home state on equal terms with the residents of the other state was protected by the privileges and immunities clause in the original Constitution, but the right to do so within the person's own state was deemed not protected by the privileges or immunities clause of the Fourteenth Amendment. The majority decision by Sutherland emphasized that one "purpose and effect" of the Fourteenth Amendment was to "bridge the gap" between those two provisions, extending and completing the "shield of national protection between the citizen and hostile and discriminating state legislation." That protection, Sutherland declared, "cannot be lightly dismissed as a mere duplication, or of subordinate or no value, or as an almost forgotten clause of the Constitution."[49] Interference with freedom of contract, the majority held, "may be a liberty safeguarded by the due process of law clause, and at the same time, none the less, a privilege protected by the privileges and immunities clause of the Fourteenth Amendment."[50]

It appeared that Sutherland was going out of his way to ground protection for economic liberty on firmer constitutional ground. But the decision did not directly take on *Slaughter-House*, nor did the outcome break new legal ground, because the burdens of the law were placed upon people conducting businesses across state lines rather than within their own state, so technically the Fourteenth Amendment was not directly implicated. As a consequence, the dissenting opinion by Justice Harlan F. Stone was fairly mild, noting that "even those basic privileges and immunities secured against federal infringement by the first eight amendments have been held not to be protected from state action by the privileges and immunities clause"[51]; and that although at least forty-four cases decided by the Supreme Court had involved challenges to state laws under the privileges or immunities clause, "[u]ntil today, none has held that state legislation infringed that clause."[52]

In any event, the exhumation of the privileges or immunities clause was short-lived. Only five years after *Colgate*, the court overruled that decision and upheld a discriminatory tax classification in

Madden v. Commonwealth of Kentucky. The seven-member majority held that "the presumption of constitutionality" of a state statute involving tax classifications "can be overcome only by the most explicit demonstration that a classification is a hostile and oppressive discrimination against particular persons and classes. The burden is on the one attacking the legislative arrangement to negative every conceivable basis which might support it."[53] Completely gone was any concern over class legislation or the burden on freedom of enterprise. Expressly embracing *Slaughter-House*, the court thought it "quite clear that the right to carry out an incident to a trade, business or calling . . . is not a privilege of national citizenship" protected by the privileges or immunities clause.[54]

Though Sutherland and his fellow conservatives put up a brave fight against New Deal statism, it was ultimately a losing one. After *West Coast Hotel Co. v. Parrish*, the court struck down no further New Deal legislation, and before long Roosevelt had replaced all of the dissenters from that opinion. That left the court free to fashion a jurisprudence that accorded protection to certain rights but not to others, such as economic liberty.

It laid the foundation to do so in a 1938 case called *U.S. v. Carolene Products Co.*, another protectionist law involving milk. The company was charged with violating a law that forbade the shipment of "filled milk," which is skimmed milk compounded with any fat or oil other than milk fat. Par for the course, a majority of the court, in an opinion by Stone, upheld the law under the deferential rational basis test that presumes the law's constitutionality.[55]

But in what has become the most famous footnote in a Supreme Court case—indeed, the footnote is better known than the substance of the decision—the court for the first time created, out of whole cloth, a pecking order for constitutional rights. The court noted that there "may be narrower scope for operation of the presumption of constitutionality when legislation appears on its face to be within a specific prohibition of the Constitution, such as those of the first ten amendments," and that "more searching judicial inquiry" may also be appropriate where a law evidences prejudice against "discrete and insular minorities."[56] Other rights, such as economic liberty, would receive less-searching scrutiny.

Thus the court embarked down the road of assigning specific groups and constitutional rights different tiers of constitutional scrutiny, from "strict," meaning the government rarely wins; to "intermediate," in which the government sometimes wins; to "rational basis," in which the government nearly always wins. That was good news for ethnic minorities and for rights such as freedom of speech, which for the first time gained robust protection by the federal courts. It was bad news for freedom of enterprise, which was relegated to the lowest tier of judicial scrutiny. It also disparaged the rule of law, because it allows judges to decide, based largely on their own subjective preferences, which rights should receive strong protection while others receive little or none; and because it means that an individual's rights depend upon whether the law is based upon a person's ethnic status or some lesser-protected type of status, such as entrepreneurs or economic competitors of those who have manipulated the law to their advantage. It is difficult to imagine that this type of judicial evolution—or, perhaps more appropriately, judicial counterrevolution—could have occurred if the court had given the privileges or immunities clause its intended meaning in *Slaughter-House*.

It also quickly became clear that the court would not protect economic liberties even where they are expressly guaranteed by the Constitution. One of the few explicit limitations on state power in the original Constitution was the Contract Clause, which prohibits states from passing any "Law impairing the Obligation of Contracts." That language is about as straightforward as it gets. For instance, even if it is within the state's power to enact a minimum-wage law, the law should apply prospectively so as not to impair existing contracts.

But in its decision in *Home Building & Loan Association v. Blaisdell*, the court upheld a Minnesota law that limited the ability of mortgage holders to foreclose loans under the terms of their contracts.[57] After *Blaisdell*, although it generally has construed the clause to prohibit states from violating their own contracts, the court has subjected laws impairing private contracts to lenient review. The result is that private businesses and individuals can make contracts that are perfectly legal today, only to have the state change the terms or completely obliterate them tomorrow—and the parties have little recourse despite the obvious intent of the Constitution's framers to prohibit states from having such power. The judiciary's recognition of a police power sweeping far beyond anything the framers would recognize, combined with the power to alter the terms of contracts after the fact, renders all contracts dependent on the whim of the government, thus undermining the sanctity of contract and the rule of law on which a free economy—indeed, a free society—depends.

The court also dispensed with crucial private property rights protected explicitly by the Fifth Amendment, which provides that private property may be taken for "public use" on the condition that just compensation is paid. In *Berman v. Parker*, the court sustained the use of eminent domain to clear a "blighted" area that included, among other non-blighted properties, a functioning department store. The store's owner argued that the Fifth Amendment did not allow the taking of his property for the benefit of a private developer. Deciding that it was appropriate for the District of Columbia to determine that the neighborhood should be "beautiful as well as sanitary,"[58] a unanimous Supreme Court amended the Fifth Amendment's language to predicate the use of eminent domain not on a showing of public *use* but on the much more forgiving requirement of public *benefit*—a quality that, like beauty, lies in the eye of the beholder. Again, this crucial change in constitutional wording occurred not through the amendment process but by judicial dictate.

The decision in *Parker* opened the floodgates to the use of eminent domain—one of government's most invasive and destructive powers—to expropriate one individual's property for the benefit of another. It laid the groundwork for the infamous decision a half century later in *Kelo v. City of New London*[59] in which the Court upheld the confiscation and demolition of a working-class neighborhood to make way for amenities for a Pfizer facility. Despite the generous bounty bestowed upon it, Pfizer eventually moved out of New London—leaving behind empty upon which tidy homes and flourishing businesses had been bulldozed.[60]

At the same time the court was narrowing protections of economic liberty, it was giving an expansive reading to constitutional sources of federal power. One of the most important powers conferred by the Constitution on the federal government is to regulate interstate commerce. The purpose was to prevent parochial trade barriers erected by states before the adoption of the Constitution. But during the New Deal, the court transformed the Commerce Clause into an open-ended authority to regulate virtually any economic activity, even if it was not involved in interstate commerce. During the Depression, Congress adopted the Agricultural Adjustment Act of 1938, which imposed limits on wheat production in order to drive up prices. A farmer, Roscoe Filburn, exceeded the limit. Despite the fact that Filburn intended to use the wheat to feed his chickens, he was ordered to pay a fine and destroy his crops. In *Wickard v. Filburn*, the Supreme Court upheld the law, reasoning that even economic activity taking place on a single farm has sufficient effect on interstate commerce to allow Congress to regulate it. After all, had Filburn obeyed the law, he would have had to buy chicken feed from someone else.[61] The tortured logic of *Wickard v. Filburn* continues to haunt us today, for it provides the rationale (however flimsy) for the imposition of an individual mandate to purchase insurance under the federal health care law.

The evolution of law described in this section mostly took place over the course of about seventy-five years following the adoption of the Fourteenth Amendment.[62] Since then, the Supreme Court has turned more conservative. Yet most of the worst decisions from the New Deal and Warren Court eras continue to govern American law. The Rehnquist Court made noteworthy progress in restoring limits in some areas, such as property rights (but not eminent domain) and the use of the Commerce Clause as a source of unbounded congressional power (although it expressly reaffirmed *Wickard v. Filburn*).[63] But the enormous promise of the Fourteenth Amendment in protecting economic liberty has remained unfulfilled. A revolutionary constitutional provision intended to clip government's wings has been relegated to the constitutional dustbin. As a result, regulation of economic activities at every level of government, including access to entry-level opportunities, is essentially limitless.

Though the emergence of the regulatory leviathan has many fathers, its forebear is the profound judicial error and abdication performed in the *Slaughter-House Cases*. As Shankman and Pilon aptly have observed,

> Had the Slaughterhouse Court properly read and applied the Privileges or Immunities Clause, we would doubtless have today a very different body of constitutional law than we have—and a very different nation, not least in the area of race relations, but not there alone. Jim Crow and the de jure segregation that characterized it would not have been permitted; but neither would the far-reaching state regulation of economic activity that came later.[64]

If we are to get our nation back on track as a beacon of enterprise, sustained by the rule of law, our sights must be fixed on toppling *Slaughter-House*.

Fortunately, that effort has begun in earnest.

PART 4

A REBIRTH FOR ECONOMIC LIBERTY

NYONE WHO HAS made it to this point can be excused for concluding that the quest to revive judicial protection for economic liberty is hopeless. Regulation, even of entry-level businesses and occupations, is ubiquitous. Industries, trade associations, and unions clamor before legislative bodies and regulatory agencies to secure favored treatment that disadvantages competitors and newcomers. No matter how oppressive or arbitrary, laws restricting economic liberty are accorded nearly complete deference by the judiciary, so much so that it is rarely worth the cost to challenge them even in the instances where those victimized by them possess the resources to do so.

Not only are the vast majority of judicial decisions hostile to economic liberty, but many of the judges who ordinarily would be most inclined to protect economic liberty exhibit as much disdain for the so-called *Lochner* era—the period between the late 1890s and mid-1930s described in the preceding section in which the U.S. Supreme Court protected economic liberty under the due process clause—as do liberals. That is because although judicial protection for economic liberty died during the New Deal, the underlying concept of "substantive due process" did not, and repeatedly it has been pressed into service by liberals, mainly to protect abortion and related rights. Many conservative scholars and jurists believe that if they revive judicial protection for economic liberty, they will implicitly sanction liberal judicial adventurism. Of course, perversely, such liberal judicial adventurism is alive and well, while economic liberty—which the framers of both the original Constitution and the Fourteenth Amendment sought to protect—is not.

When I think of a proper metaphor for the state of judicial protection for economic liberty today, what comes to mind is the hapless knight in *Monty Python and the Holy Grail* who, having had all his limbs severed, nonetheless insists that he will carry on the fight because it's merely a "flesh wound" and he isn't dead yet. I also think of my dear friend and hero Milton Friedman who was asked shortly after the millennium whether he was disappointed in the slow pace for school choice, an idea to which his writings gave birth fifty years earlier. He replied that given that nothing at all had happened in the first forty years, even the slight progress during the most recent ten years seemed remarkable. Drawing from those analogies, perhaps it's accurate to say that although economic liberty experienced a pretty tough century and a third, lately, by comparison, things aren't looking quite so bad.

When I began examining this state of affairs during law school and early in my career, the only scholar who had written anything recently on the topic was University of San Diego law professor Bernard Siegan, whose 1981 book, *Economic Liberties and the Constitution*,[1] was a clarion call to me. Shortly thereafter, University of Chicago law professor Richard Epstein wrote his towering work, *Takings*,[2] examining the theoretical underpinnings of the eminent domain clause and applying them to challenge the regulatory welfare state in creative ways. Before long, conservatives and libertarians, despite an overwhelming numerical disadvantage, seized the offensive in legal scholarship. They no longer merely railed against liberal excesses and judicial excesses, but breathed new life into discarded constitutional doctrines and provisions, such as federalism, the Ninth Amendment, and the privileges or immunities clause.[3]

The emergence of this intellectual challenge to the jurisprudential status quo—what some on the Left have referred to disparagingly as the Constitution-in-Exile movement—was not entirely accidental. Although the Nixon administration was in part a consequence of the excesses of the Supreme Court under Chief Justice Earl Warren, Nixon's strategy to remake the judiciary was haphazard, and only accidentally produced the inspired appointment of Justice (later Chief Justice) William H. Rehnquist. But President Ronald Reagan, supported by Attorney General Edwin Meese and other key Justice Department officials such as Charles Cooper and Michael Carvin (with whom I was lucky enough to serve at a formative stage in my legal career), had a deliberate and determined strategy to appoint justices and judges committed to the doctrine of original intent.

At the same time, one of the most seminal developments in modern jurisprudence took place: the creation in the 1980s of the Federalist Society. Initially begun to counter the liberal influence in legal academia, the Federalist Society quickly spread to law schools across the United States. Reagan administration lawyers were key leaders and advisors. Although its membership spans the broad philosophical spectrum between libertarian Richard Epstein and conservative Robert Bork, the Federalist Society is united by a devotion to the rule of law and original intent. By the time of the two Bush administrations, the Federalist Society's influence had grown so great that it was able to help ensure the appointment of judges and justices who would continue and advance the Reagan jurisprudential legacy.

As well, a number of conservative public interest law firms began to emerge. Initially, they were geographically oriented, such as Pacific Legal Foundation in Sacramento, while later groups began to focus on specific issues, such as the Institute for Justice in Arlington, Va., which I co-founded with Chip Mellor in 1991 to litigate in such

areas as school choice, economic liberty, private property rights, and
the First Amendment. Such groups generated the financial resources
to take on cases that could not have been litigated otherwise. Com-
bining well-crafted test cases with legal theories developed by conservative and libertarian legal scholars, several of the groups have
achieved significant legal victories.[4]

As the court began to grow more conservative, it issued some
decisions making the lenient "rational basis" test more robust in certain contexts. In *City of Cleburne v. Cleburne Living Center*, the court
invalidated the city's requirement of a special use permit for a home
for mentally retarded persons. The court began with the proposi-
tion that the equal protection clause is a "direction that all persons
similarly situated should be treated alike."[5] In a departure from the
usual rule of blind deference to government action, the court applied rational basis scrutiny to require the government to show that
the group affected adversely by the law possesses "distinguishing
characteristics" that justify a "distinctive legislative response" and
that the law actually is "based on [that] distinction."[6] Many instances
of governmental line-drawing would not be able to survive such an
analysis.

The court applied a similar analysis under the due process clause
in *Moore v. City of East Cleveland*, in which the court struck down a
zoning ordinance limiting occupancy of dwelling units to members
of a nuclear family, thus prohibiting a grandmother from living with
her grandson. Writing for a plurality of four justices, Justice Lewis
F. Powell stated that with regard to liberties protected by the due
process clause, the court "must examine carefully the importance of
the governmental interests advanced and the extent to which they
are served by the challenged regulation."[7] Acknowledging that the
city's concerns about congestion, overcrowding, and demand on city
services were "legitimate," Powell nonetheless concluded that the law
served those objectives "marginally, at best."[8] Powell did not define
the full range of liberties protected by the due process clause, but
quoted Justice Harlan's definition of liberty as "a rational continuum

which, broadly speaking, includes a freedom from all substantial arbitrary impositions and purposeless restraints."[9] Powell concluded, "Appropriate limits on substantive due process come not from drawing arbitrary lines but rather from careful 'respect for the teachings of history [and] solid recognition of the basic values that underlie our society'."[10] Of course, economic liberty fits neatly into that definition.

Meanwhile, although the courts during the Reagan era were silent on the privileges or immunities clause of the Fourteenth Amendment, they were vigilant in restricting discriminatory economic regulations among states under the privileges and immunities clause of Article IV, section 2, and the Commerce Clause. Indeed, in one 1984 case, the Supreme Court proclaimed that "the pursuit of a common calling is one of the most fundamental" of the privileges and immunities protected by the original Constitution.[11] Combined with a handful of other cases that remained viable precedents—such as the *Yick Wo* decision striking down the San Francisco ordinance restricting laundry businesses—these precedents provided a basis for courts to more closely examine discriminatory, arbitrary, or burdensome regulations of economic liberty.

This was the climate in which I began challenging barriers to enterprise in 1987, equipped with a handful of encouraging legal precedents, an emerging body of legal scholarship, and an increasingly receptive federal judiciary. And yet the enormousness of adverse precedent was daunting. The strategy my colleagues and I developed in light of the enormous odds was four-fold: (1) bring cases with sympathetic clients, outrageous abuses, and heinous villains; (2) argue narrow and modest legal theories, relying on equal protection and due process until the time was ripe to confront *Slaughter-House* in the U.S. Supreme Court; (3) argue our cases not only in the courts of law but in the court of public opinion, building the ethos of economic liberty that Justice Scalia had called for; and (4) develop plenty of stamina, because losses would be frequent and painful, and the task of restoring economic liberty could take decades and might not succeed at all.

Heeding Scalia's advice, I looked for a launch case that would personify the constitutional ethos of economic liberty. I found it in, of all places, the pages of the *Washington Post* Sunday magazine. It told the story of Ego Brown, a former government bureaucrat who longed to go into business for himself. He found a market niche in the thousands of scuffed shoes pounding the pavement of the streets of the nation's capital. He cashed in his pension, bought a shoeshine stand, and set up business at the corner of Nineteenth and M streets.

Business thrived. The flamboyant Brown clad himself in a tuxedo and enticed customers to purchase an "Ego Shine." Business was so good that social workers began referring enterprising homeless people to him. He would set them up with a shoe shine stand and a tuxedo, giving them, as he put it, a hand up rather than a handout.

But in Washington, D.C., no good deed goes unpunished. The District dusted off an old Jim Crow-era law that forbade bootblacks on public streets, and police were dispatched to shut his business down.

When I met Ego Brown, he was shining shoes as a hotel employee, his dream of owning his own business put on hold. I told him his civil rights had been violated and that I would like to represent him for free. I had little litigation experience and my legal theories were un-tested, but my price was right.

While the litigation went on, the hotel where Ego Brown was shin-ing shoes closed down for renovations. He lost his job. Before long, Brown was nearly destitute, and the utility company threatened to cut off his heat. My friend Robert Woodson, the visionary founder of the National Center for Neighborhood Enterprise, threw him a rent party and Ego and his family made it through the winter.

On the first day of spring in 1989, the federal district court did a very peculiar thing: it became one of the first federal courts in about fifty years to strike down an economic regulation as a violation of the Fourteenth Amendment. Declaring that "the rational basis test re-quires that the justification posited by the legislature be *both* conceiv-able and rational,"[12] the court found that the "inability of the District to articulate any rational basis for distinguishing bootblacks from other types of vendors combined with the regulation's elusive purpose compel us to declare this regulation unconstitutional."[13]

The *Brown* decision became the first solid building block in the effort to build jurisprudence favorable to economic liberty. But in addition to the milestone legal victory, another equally important development happened as well. Ego Brown's story caught the fancy of the media. And after he won his case, Brown was made "Person of the Week" on ABC's *World News Tonight.* I will never forget Peter Jennings's closing words about Ego: "He's made us all a little bit freer." The effort to restore the ethos of economic liberty had begun.

The next victory was a case I litigated against the Houston Anti-Jitney Law of 1924. In the 1920s, the two main means of public transportation were jitneys—motorized vehicles operating on fixed routes for a flat fee, without government subsidies—and streetcars. Unable to beat the competition in the marketplace, streetcar companies went from city to city to get jitneys banned. By the late twentieth century, although streetcars were long gone in most cities, the anti-jitney laws remained, kept in place by other public transit monopolies.

A Houston taxicab driver, Alfredo Santos, encountered the Anti-Jitney Law when he tried to start a jitney business using his off-duty cab. The business model was ideal: he could pick the busiest travel corridors and times, travel a fixed route, yet pick up and discharge passengers wherever they wished, and charge much less than the public transit system, with no taxpayer subsidies. Of course, such entrepreneurship was intolerable to the city, which shut down Santos's jitney business.

But the federal district court saw things differently. Judge John D. Rainey found that the "purpose of the statute was economic protectionism in its most glaring form, and this goal was not legitimate." Moreover, even if the goal were legitimate, "the ordinance has long out-lived its ill-begotten existence."[14] Hence, the law flunked both parts of the rational basis test.

There were unsuccessful lawsuits as well. I litigated another case against the District of Columbia, challenging its cosmetology licensing laws. At the time, virtually every state had laws compelling anyone who worked with hair to obtain a barbering or cosmetology license. The licensing boards were comprised of members of the regulated businesses, who were in charge of composing the required curriculum and testing requirements.

The District of Columbia applied its cosmetology licensing law to shut down a thriving salon called Cornrows & Co., owned by two young entrepreneurs, Taalib-din Uqdah and Pamela Ferrell. The salon provided only one service: the intricate, centuries-old art of African hair-braiding. Neither the prescribed 1,600-hour curriculum (more than the hours necessary to become a police officer or an emergency medical technician) nor the licensing examination included any training or demonstrated proficiency in African hairstyling. They did, however, mandate extensive training and demonstrated proficiency in all manner of services that Cornrows & Co. did not provide: the use of chemicals (including hair straightening, which is highly offensive to African hairstylists), cosmetics, eyebrow arching, and nail painting.

A more ridiculous regulatory mismatch between purported public health and safety objectives and the actual requirements would be difficult to imagine. Yet, when the case went to court, although the federal judge was overtly sympathetic, he concluded that under the rational basis test he was compelled to sustain the law.[15]

At around the same time, my colleagues were litigating Leroy Jones's case against the taxicab monopoly in Denver, Colorado (described in Part 1). As in the Uqdah case, the federal judge concluded that under the rational basis test, there was nothing he could do to bring down the barriers that separated Jones and his colleagues from fulfillment of their entrepreneurial aspirations.[16]

But fortunately, while both cases were pending on appeal, the battles were won in the court of public opinion. Previously, the entrepreneurs in both cases had no chance to prevail in the political arena against the powerful special interests wielding vast resources to preserve the status quo. But with the light of media sunshine and an outpouring of public support, the economic barriers fell. Editorials in the *Wall Street Journal*, a typically scathing expose of the District of Columbia cosmetology cartel by television journalist John Stossel, and a CBS "Eye on America" segment on Leroy Jones's fight against the Denver taxicab oligopoly combined with local media to pressure the District of Columbia to deregulate African hairstyling and the state of Colorado to deregulate entry into the taxicab market in Denver.

Today, there are dozens of African hairstyling salons (including Cornrows & Co.) operating in the nation's capital, providing scores of employment opportunities and substantial tax revenues while operating in the economic mainstream rather than in the underground economy. In the midst of the Denver battle, Jones and his colleagues realized their fight had broad ramifications; they renamed their company Freedom Cabs. Today, dozens of purple Freedom Cabs provide transportation to Colorado residents and visitors along with the opportunity for co-op members to own their own businesses.

Subsequent cases have seen generally greater success in court. Following the unsuccessful challenge to cosmetology regulations in the District of Columbia, I took on California's licensing scheme on behalf of African hairstylists there. In his 1999 decision in *Cornwell v. Hamilton* striking down the rules, federal district court Judge Rudi M. Brewster declared that under the rational basis test, "[t]here must be some congruity between the means employed and the stated end or the test would be a nullity."[17] Sifting meticulously through the regulations, curriculum, and examination, the court found only a tiny fraction applied to African hairstyling, thus failing to satisfy the necessary nexus between public health and safety objectives and the rules. Following the *Cornwell* decision, legislators in other states began deregulating African hairstyling, removing cartel-backed obstacles to economic opportunity.

The Institute for Justice filed a pair of challenges against regulations procured by another pernicious cartel: the funeral home industry, which supported laws in numerous states making it unlawful to directly sell caskets to consumers, thus driving up prices and forcing purchases at a time of great emotional distress for many families.

The U.S. Court of Appeals for the Sixth Circuit could find no connection between Tennessee's purported objectives and its ban on direct casket sales to consumers by businesses other than funeral homes. As a result, wrote Judge Danny Boggs, "we are left with the more obvious illegitimate purpose to which the licensure provision is very well tailored"—specifically, limiting competition in the casket market.[18] A law "to privilege certain businessmen over others at the expense of consumers," the court concluded, "is not animated by a legitimate governmental purpose and cannot survive even rational basis review."[19]

Faced with the same scenario only two years later, the Tenth Circuit produced the opposite result, holding (remarkably) that "protecting or favoring one particular intrastate industry, absent a specific federal constitutional or statutory violation, is a legitimate state interest."[20] While acknowledging that "dishing out special economic benefits to certain in-state industries remains the favored pastime of state and local governments," the court expressed fear that a rule forbidding economic protectionism would constitute a "threat to all licensed professions such as doctors, teachers, accountants, plumbers, electricians, and lawyers" (gasp, even *lawyers*?!), and that "every piece of legislation . . . aiming to protect or favor one industry or business over another in the hopes of luring jobs to that state would be in danger." The court concluded that while "such a libertarian paradise may be a worthy goal, Plaintiffs must turn to the Oklahoma electorate for its institution, not us."[21]

The plaintiffs in the Oklahoma casket case were not seeking a libertarian paradise but recourse to the basic rule of law. Indeed, it was precisely the power to snuff out economic liberty that the framers of the Fourteenth Amendment intended to curb. A legislature cannot be a fair judge of whether economic legislation truly advances legitimate health and safety objectives as opposed to advancing the self-serving objectives of special-interest groups. The difference between the Sixth and Tenth Circuit decisions on precisely that question is stark: the Sixth Circuit believes the courts can and should perform such an analysis, while the Tenth Circuit believes the courts should not do so and that it doesn't matter anyway, because it is within the legislative prerogative to advance economic protectionism for favored industries.

Given that the Fourteenth Amendment's framers intended not only the privileges or immunities clause but also the equal protection guarantee to prevent such special-interest legislation, this issue should not remotely be in dispute. Yet it is a testament to the erosion of judicial protection for economic liberty that this threshold issue is very much an open question.

It is a question that only the U.S. Supreme Court can resolve. But despite the irreconcilable clash between two federal courts of appeals, the Supreme Court decided not to review the Tenth Circuit's decision in the Oklahoma casket case, so that in one circuit some semblance of economic freedom prevails, while in the other it does not.

The most recent significant economic liberty decision straddled the divide between the Sixth and Tenth circuits. In *Merrifield v. Lockyer*, litigated by Pacific Legal Foundation attorney Timothy Sandefur, the plaintiff challenged California's licensing scheme that imposed pesticide testing requirements on pest control businesses that did not use pesticides. Moreover, the scheme exempted certain types of non-pesticide-using businesses. As Sandefur points out, "if Merrifield installed a screen on a building to keep a raccoon out, he did not need a license, but if he installed the *same* screen on the *same* building to keep a *rat* out, he needed to spend two years learning to use pesticides and take a difficult and time-consuming test about the lifespan of insects and the dangers of chemical poisons."[22]

In a decision by Judge Diarmuid O'Scannlain, the Ninth Circuit affirmed the overall requirement for testing about pesticides even as to pest control businesses that do not use pesticides. However, it held that the exemption for certain pest controllers flunked the rational basis test. In so doing, the Ninth Circuit agreed with the Sixth Circuit holding in *Craigmiles* that "mere economic protectionism for the sake of economic protectionism is irrational with respect to determining if a classification survives rational basis review," but stated that "there might be instances when economic protectionism might be related to a legitimate governmental interest."[23] This three-way split among circuit courts increases the odds that the U.S. Supreme Court will address the question before long.

Indeed, it may have a chance to do just that in the context of yet another case involving direct sales of caskets to consumers, this time by a group of monks.[24] The monks at St. Joseph Abbey in Covington, Louisiana, have for years made caskets from lumber produced from their pine forest. But after Hurricane Katrina pummeled much of the forest, they decided to sell caskets to the public, at lower prices than are charged by funeral homes, in order to support the abbey. Even though the monks sold only sixty caskets since 2007 in a state in which about 40,000 people die each year, the specter of competition was too much for the funeral home industry, which turned back legislative efforts to repeal its state-imposed monopoly and urged the State Board of Embalmers and Funeral Directors to take action against the monks. The board obliged, and the monks are subject to up to 180 days in jail and fines of as much as $2,500 for each violation. A federal lawsuit was filed on August 12, 2010, challenging the cartel. The monks' case will invite yet another court of appeals (the Fifth Circuit) to weigh in. If the case eventually reaches the Supreme Court, it could either bury economic liberty once and for all or exhume it from jurisprudential purgatory.

As numerous economic liberty cases resulted in divergent outcomes in the lower courts, the Supreme Court began to signal that it might have an interest in revisiting *Slaughter-House* or at least in expanding the scope of the privileges or immunities clause. In 1999, the court decided a case called *Saenz v. Roe*, which involved California's system of paying lower welfare benefits for one year to people who moved from other states that had lower benefits, to reduce the incentive to move to California for higher payments.

This scenario put the liberal justices in a bit of a bind. The state was discriminating against individuals after they had become residents. The equal protection clause would offer little assistance: because the law affected neither a suspect classification nor fundamental rights, it would trigger only rational basis scrutiny, and certainly California had a rational basis for the law.

So seven justices—the four liberal justices plus Sandra Day O'Connor, Antonin Scalia, and Anthony Kennedy—sought a solution in the privileges or immunities clause. Certainly the right to welfare benefits was not among the privileges or immunities intended to be protected by the clause. But a majority of the court held that the "right to travel" was protected as part of an individual's national citizenship.[25] By so holding, the court was able to apply a "categorical" rule against discrimination based on length of domicile, rather than the rational basis test.[26]

Dissenting, Justice Clarence Thomas took the opportunity to call upon the court to correct its grievous jurisprudential error in *Slaughter-House*. With regard to a right to welfare benefits, Thomas observed that "the majority attributes a meaning to the Privileges or Immunities Clause that likely was unintended when the Fourteenth Amendment was enacted and ratified."[27] He urged the court to "look to history to ascertain the original meaning of the Clause," noting that "[l]egal scholars agree on little beyond the conclusion that the Clause does not mean what the Court said it meant" in *Slaughter-House*.[28] "Although the majority appears to breathe new life into the Clause today," he observed, "it fails to address its historical underpinnings or its place in our constitutional jurisprudence." He concluded that because "the demise of the Privileges or Immunities Clause has contributed in no small part to the current disarray of our Fourteenth Amendment jurisprudence, I would be open to reevaluating its meaning in an appropriate case."[29]

Saenz was the first time since the adoption of the Fourteenth Amendment (apart from the short-lived decision in *Colgate v. Harvey*, discussed in Part 3) in which the court struck down a statute as a violation of the privileges or immunities clause. Given that eight justices agreed that the clause has substantive effect against the states (only Chief Justice Rehnquist appeared to believe the clause has no meaning), the door now appeared open to reinvigorate the clause, as Thomas suggested, "in an appropriate case."

The next opportunity would come about a decade later. In 2008, the Supreme Court decided for the first time in *District of Columbia v. Heller*[30] that the Second Amendment protects an individual's right to keep and bear arms. But because the case involved a District of Columbia ordinance and not a law made by a state or one of its subdivisions, the court had no occasion to consider whether the Second Amendment applied to the states through the Fourteenth Amendment. That occasion would occur soon thereafter in *McDonald v. City of Chicago*.

Following the *Cruikshank* decision discussed in the preceding section, the Second Amendment had not been applied to the states pursuant to the doctrine of "selective incorporation" of the Bill of Rights through the Fourteenth Amendment's due process clause. Given the Court's decision in *Heller*, however, it was highly likely that the court would find in *McDonald* that the Second Amendment applied to the states.

But the question was how. Attorney Alan Gura, a former Institute for Justice law clerk who argued both cases, was determined to convince the court to abandon its incoherent selective incorporation jurisprudence, to apply the Second Amendment to the states through the privileges or immunities clause rather than due process, and perhaps to overturn *Slaughter-House* for good measure. A remarkable portion of the many briefs submitted on both sides addressed the privileges or immunities clause.

But the Supreme Court typically makes evolutionary, not revolutionary, changes to the law. Though Gura devoted much of his argument to the privileges or immunities clause, he was met with pointed skepticism from both conservative and liberal justices who wanted to know why it was necessary to overturn *Slaughter-House.*[31] They were right: simply by extending its jurisprudence, the court could apply the Second Amendment to the states through the due process clause. It is only to protect economic liberty that the holding of *Slaughter-House* needs squarely to be addressed.

Ultimately, the court took the easier route of the due process clause to hold that the right to keep and bear arms applies to the states. But the court's opinion by Justice Samuel Alito respectfully considered the privileges or immunities argument in a way that gives hope to those who might raise the issue in the future. "The constitutional Amendments adopted in the aftermath of the Civil War fundamentally altered our country's federal system," Alito declared.[32] He observed that "many legal scholars dispute the correctness of the narrow *Slaughter-House* interpretation" of the privileges or immunities clause.[33] But Alito concluded that "petitioners are unable to identify the Clause's full scope," nor "is there any consensus on that question among the scholars who agree that the *Slaughter-House Cases*' interpretation is flawed." As a result, and given that the court simply could extend incorporation of the Bill of Rights through the due process clause, Alito concluded that "[w]e see no need to reconsider" *Slaughter-House* in that case.[34]

As he did in *Saenz*, Thomas went much further in his concurring opinion, this time presenting a brilliant fifty-six-page exposition of the history and intent of the privileges or immunities clause and a sweeping indictment of the court's jurisprudence since *Slaughter-House.* Although Thomas agreed that the Second Amendment's protection of the individual right to keep and bear arms is incorporated through the Fourteenth Amendment, "I cannot agree that it is enforceable against the States through a clause that speaks only to 'process'."[35] Properly understood, Thomas concluded, the privileges or immunities clause "establishes a minimum baseline of federal rights."[36] The "mere fact that the Clause does not expressly list the rights it protects does not render it incapable of principled judicial application," he declared. "I believe those questions are far more worthy of this Court's attention—and far more likely to yield discernable answers—than the substantive due process questions the Court has for years created on its own, with neither textual nor historical support."[37]

Thomas's opinion is the most scathing condemnation of *Slaughter-House* ever written by a contemporary Supreme Court justice. It also makes for delightful and inspiring reading. And far from closing the door to reconsidering *Slaughter-House,* Alito's opinion—joined in part by Thomas and in its entirety by Chief Justice John Roberts and Justices Scalia and Kennedy—more sharply questioned its underpinnings than has any other majority decision by the court.

So it appears that an invitation exists for the court to reconsider *Slaughter-House* in the right circumstances. Plainly, anyone taking on *Slaughter-House* will have to come equipped to explain to the court's satisfaction the full scope of the privileges or immunities clause, a task to which I hope this book will contribute.

That is a vitally important task. A majority of the current Supreme Court appears to agree that the privileges or immunities clause means something more than nothing—and, significantly, more than it was interpreted to mean in *Slaughter-House.* But the court does not appear prepared to open a Pandora's box. It would rather hew to the narrow content of the clause ascribed to it in *Slaughter-House* than to create a new empty vessel for previously unknown constitutional rights.

Despite disagreements among scholars over the exact contours of the clause, the strong weight of historical evidence indicates that privileges or immunities, at the time of the adoption of the Fourteenth Amendment, were meant to encompass rights that existed at common law, rights protected by the U.S. Constitution (including the Bill of Rights in its entirety), and rights protected by the Civil Rights Act of 1866. As the framers of the Fourteenth Amendment repeatedly suggested, the definition of privileges or immunities is very broad. But it is not boundless. Indeed, the rights protected at common law, in the Constitution, and in the Civil Rights Act of 1866 overlap greatly. In areas of the law ranging from property to contracts, courts frequently examine the origins and particulars of common law rights. Of course, freedom of enterprise was protected under common law, and it was the core of the Civil Rights Act of 1866. By contrast, judicially recognized rights of more recent vintage were not protected under common law. If a right was established at the time of the adoption of the Fourteenth Amendment, it is protected as a privilege or immunity of citizenship; if it was not so recognized, it is not protected under that clause. That line of demarcation is a significant limitation on the content of protected privileges or immunities.

But carefully defining the scope of privileges or immunities is not the only constraint on judicial adventurism. As the *Slaughter-House* dissenters recognized, the privileges or immunities clause was not meant to constrain proper exercises of the states' police power. All of the dissenters readily conceded that the portions of the challenged law addressing sanitary concerns were valid. But based on abundant experience, the framers of the Fourteenth Amendment did not trust legislatures to draw lines between individuals to whom economic opportunities were given and those from whom they were withheld. Hence the appropriate judicial inquiry would focus on whether a particular constraint on economic activity advances a legitimate police power or does not.

Such an inquiry is not about the wisdom of policy decisions, but their purpose and effect. Such a task was skillfully undertaken (not to make a pun) by the Sixth Circuit in the Tennessee casket case. For instance, regulations of taxicab licenses to require insurance, safety, honesty, transparency, and driving knowledge all would easily be sustained; an oligopoly allowing no new entrants into the business since World War II would not.

Unlike the legislative arena, in which special-interest groups have both the incentive and resources to affect such line-drawing—and even much more so in the administrative arena, which often is even more susceptible to special-interest influence—in the judicial arena, both sides have the ability to present evidence on equal terms. Insulated from democratic pressures, the judiciary is far more impartial and objective than the executive and legislative branches can or were intended to be. The judicial enterprise charted by the *Slaughter-House* dissenters is far more modest than goes on every day in such areas as First Amendment infringements and racial classifications, or even in non-constitutional areas of law such as tort law, contract interpretation, and application of criminal statutes. Yet even modest judicial review would yield far greater protection to freedom of enterprise than has existed for the past seventy-five years. The bottom line is that whatever the fear of runaway judges, which not only conservative but liberal commentators have viewed with alarm, it is nothing compared to runaway legislative and administrative bodies that have cut off the bottom rungs of the economic ladder.

Even if the Supreme Court never expressly overturns *Slaughter-House*, it may well be responsive to reconsidering jurisprudence that relegates economic liberty to the lowest level of judicial protection. As it continues to make the rational basis test more robust in other contexts—most recently, in protecting the rights of homosexuals[38]— it should appear increasingly discordant not to do so in the context of economic liberty.

As the ground for a revival of judicial protection for freedom of enterprise grows more fertile, advocates for economic liberty are expanding their legal strategies. In 2007, I was asked to lead the Goldwater Institute's Scharf-Norton Center for Constitutional Litigation, which focuses primarily on vindicating individual rights guarantees of the Arizona Constitution. (Other state-based public policy groups subsequently have followed the Goldwater Institute's lead in creating their own litigation centers.) For all their reverence for federalism, conservative and libertarian lawyers have focused almost entirely on the U.S. Constitution. State constitutions often contain provisions unknown to the federal constitution (such as anti-subsidy clauses). Even where they contain provisions similar to the federal Constitution, they can be interpreted more broadly.[39] State courts often look to other state courts to help interpret their own constitutions, so state constitutional precedents often have influence beyond their state boundaries.

Applying provisions of state constitutions, courts often have given greater protection to economic liberty than have federal courts.[40] One of the principal goals of the Goldwater Institute is to build upon those precedents as well as federal precedents, challenging barriers to enterprise under both the federal and state constitutions.

The first example of this hybrid strategy is the case of Cindy Vong, which currently is in litigation in Arizona state courts.[41] Vong emigrated from Vietnam as a young girl and acquired United States citizenship. She started a nail salon in Gilbert, Arizona, in 2006. Thereafter, she encountered a service called spa fish therapy, which is popular in Asian countries and elsewhere. The therapy involves clients placing their feet in a tank filled with garra rufa fish—tiny carp that have no teeth—which nibble dead skin from the feet and, reportedly, provide a relaxing experience.

Vong invested tens of thousands of dollars in fish and equipment, established sanitary standards, and opened the spa fish business in her salon. The service was so popular, with customers coming from as far as other states, that business boomed and Vong had to hire extra staff.

During a routine inspection of her nail salon by the Arizona Board of Cosmetology, Vong was questioned about the spa fish therapy. In discussions with board officials, Vong offered to operate for a trial period so the board could gather evidence as to whether the therapy was safe and sanitary. But faced with a service that it could not comprehend, and one that could pose a competitive threat to other practitioners, the board responded by ordering Vong to close the business. Faced with the prospect of losing her nail salon license and livelihood, Vong removed all of the spa fish equipment from her salon and laid off her extra staffers in the midst of a recession.

It is more than ironic that a person who fled communist oppression with her family would encounter an onerous—some might say fishy—economic obstacle in the United States. But her circumstances are emblematic of the erosion of economic liberty in America.

In November 2009, the Goldwater Institute filed suit against the director of the Board of Cosmetology, alleging violations of

Cindy Vong's economic liberty under the United States and Arizona constitutions. While the case is pending, Vong struggles to earn a living. Hers could be the case that makes it up to the U.S. Supreme Court. If not, there are many other victims of government-erected regulatory obstacles who will step forward in an effort to vindicate one of our nation's most sacred, yet least-protected, rights.

In the meantime, Vong and other entrepreneurs who have stood up for their rights teach us all a valuable lesson about the importance of the rule of law and our individual rights. Just as Rosa Parks refused to take a seat in the back of the bus and became an icon in the battle for equal rights, so are Cindy Vong and Ego Brown and Alfredo Santos and Leroy Jones and others taking their place in the pantheon of Americans who refuse to cede their economic liberty.

The battle was won more than a century ago in the aftermath of a civil war at whose core was a contest over basic human rights. Yet quickly thereafter the battle was lost again. Armed with knowledge, passion, and commitment to principle, we can win the battle to restore economic liberty once and for all. Our nation's endurance as a beacon of freedom depends on it.

▌NOTES

Introduction and Acknowledgments

1. 83 U.S. 36 (1873).

2. Antonin Scalia, "Economic Affairs as Human Affairs," in James A. Dorn and Henry G. Manne, eds., *Economic Liberties and the Judiciary* (Fairfax, VA: George Mason University Press, 1987), p. 37.

Part I: The Sorry State of Economic Liberty

1. See S. David Young, *The Rule of Experts: Occupational Licensing in America* (Washington, DC: Cato Institute, 1987).

2. Walter Williams, *The State Against Blacks* (New York: McGraw-Hill Book Co., 1982), p. 125.

3. Stuart Dorsey, "The Occupational Licensing Queue," *Journal of Human Resources*, vol. 15 (Summer 1980), p. 425.

4. Timothy Sandefur, *The Right to Earn a Living: Economic Freedom and the Law* (Washington, DC: Cato Institute, 2010), p. 17.

5. Quoted in Sandefur, *The Right to Earn a Living*, p. 18.

6. Adam Smith, *The Wealth of Nations*, quoted in *Slaughter-House Cases*, 83 U.S. at 110 n.39 (Field, J., dissenting).

7. Quoted in Sandefur, *The Right to Earn a Living*, p. 24.

8. 348 U.S. 483, 487 (1955).

9. 427 U.S. 297, 303 (1976).

10. 508 U.S. 307, 313 (1993).

11. *Id.*, 508 U.S. at 314–15.

12. *Id.*, 508 U.S. at 315 (citation omitted).

13. *Id.*, 508 U.S. at 315.

14. *Id.*, 508 U.S. at 315.

15. *Id.*, 508 U.S. at 313.

Part 2: Slaughter-House

1. Michael Kent Curtis, *No State Shall Abridge: The Fourteenth Amendment and the Bill of Rights* (Durham, NC: Duke University Press, 1986), p. 36.

2. Report of Major General Carl Schurz on Condition of the South, 39th Cong., 1st Sess., 1865, Senate Exec. Doc. No. 2, p. 24; reproduced in Alfred Avins, ed., *The Reconstruction Amendments' Debates* (Wilmington, DE: Delaware Law School, 1974), p. 90.

3. Cong. Globe, 39th Cong., 1st Sess., 1866, H. pp. 1151–52.

4. Cong. Globe, 39th Cong., 1st Sess., 1866, H. p. 1833.

5. Quoted in Michael Kent Curtis, "The Fourteenth Amendment: Recalling What the Court Forgot," 56 *Drake Law Review* 911, 986 (2008).

6. The image of House Speaker Nancy Pelosi and her colleagues scoffing at the notion of bounded national power in the context of national health-care legislation comes to mind as a jarring juxtaposition of how much the nature and quality of congressional debate have deteriorated in the past century and a half.

7. Curtis, *No State Shall Abridge*, p. 41.

8. Curtis, *No State Shall Abridge*, p. 62.

9. Curtis, "The Fourteenth Amendment," p. 925.

10. Kenyon D. Bunch, "The Original Understanding of the Privileges and Immunities Clause: Michael Perry's Justification for Judicial Activism or Robert Bork's Constitutional Inkblot?" 10 *Seton Hall Constitutional Law Journal* 321, 332 (2000).

11. Kimberly C. Shankman and Roger Pilon, "Reviving the Privileges or Immunities Clause to Redress the Balance Among States, Individuals, and the Federal Government," 3 *Texas Review of Law and Politics* 1, 7 (1998).

12. Curtis, *No State Shall Abridge*, p. 64.

13. *McDonald v. City of Chicago*, No. 08–1521 (June 28, 2010), slip op. at 9 (Thomas, J., concurring in part and concurring in the judgment).

14. *Id.* at 17 (Thomas, J.).

15. 6 F. Cas. 546, 551–52 (C.C.E.D. Penn. 1825).

16. Cong. Globe, 42nd Cong., 2nd Sess., 1872, S. p. 843.

17. Cong. Globe, 42nd Cong., 1st Sess., 1871, H. p. app. 86.

18. Cong. Globe, 43rd Cong., 1st Sess., 1874, S. p. app. 363.

19. Cong. Globe, 42nd Cong., 2nd Sess., 1872, S. p. 762.

20. Curtis, "The Fourteenth Amendment," pp. 927–28.

21. Joseph Tussman and Jacobus tenBroek, "The Equal Protection of the Laws," 37 *California Law Review* 341, 342 (1949).

22. Ronald M. Labbe and Jonathan Lurie, *The Slaughterhouse Cases: Regulation, Reconstruction, and the Fourteenth Amendment* (Lawrence, KS: University Press of Kansas, 2005), p. 15. The authors describe the conditions at length. See *id.*, pp. 12–23.

23. Charles A. Lofgren, *The Plessy Case: A Legal-Historical Interpretation* (New York: Oxford University Press, 1987), p. 67. Lofgren persuasively traces the origins of the infamous *Plessy v. Ferguson* decision to the *Slaughter-House Cases*.

24. Shankman and Pilon, "Reviving the Privileges or Immunities Clause," p. 28.

25. All biographical notes on the justices derive from Wikipedia.com.

26. Labbe and Lurie, *The Slaughterhouse Cases*, pp. 115 and 118.

27. *Slaughter-House*, 83 U.S. at 67.

28. *Id.*, 83 U.S. at 71.

29. *Id.*, 83 U.S. at 78–81.

30. *Id.*, 83 U.S. at 77.

31. Cong. Globe, 43rd Cong., 1st Sess., 1874, S. p. 3454.

32. *McDonald* at 6 (majority).

33. *Slaughter-House*, 83 U.S. at 78.

34. *Id.*, 83 U.S. at 78.

35. Labbe and Lurie, *The Slaughterhouse Cases*, p. 152.

36. Curtis, *No State Shall Abridge*, p. 173.

37. Quoted in Philip B. Kurland, "The Privileges or Immunities Clause: 'Its Hour Come Round at Last'?" 1972 *Wash. U. L. Q.* 405, 413 (1972).

38. Labbe and Lurie, *The Slaughterhouse Cases*, p. 156.

39. *Slaughter-House*, 83 U.S. at 87 (Field, J., dissenting).

40. *Id.*, 83 U.S. at 88 (Field, J.).

41. *Id.*, 83 U.S. at 101 (Field, J.).

42. *Id.*, 83 U.S. at 104 (Field, J.).

43. *Id.*, 83 U.S. at 88–89 (Field, J.).

44. *Id.*, 83 U.S. at 89 (Field, J.).

45. *Id.*, 83 U.S. at 93 (Field, J.).

46. *Id.*, 83 U.S. at 101 (Field, J.).

47. *Id.*, 83 U.S. at 96 (Field, J.).

48. *Id.*, 83 U.S. at 110 (Field, J.).

49. *Id.*, 83 U.S. at 114 (Bradley, J., dissenting).

50. *Id.*, 83 U.S. at 114 (Bradley, J.).

51. *Id.*, 83 U.S. at 112 (Bradley, J.).

52. *Id.*, 83 U.S. at 119–20 (Bradley, J.).

53. *Id.*, 83 U.S. at 129 (Swayne, J., dissenting).

54. *Id.*, 83 U.S. at 124 (Swayne, J.).

55. *Id.*, 83 U.S. at 128 (Swayne, J.).

56. *Id.*, 83 U.S. at 125 (Swayne, J.).

57. *Id.*, 83 U.S. at 129 (Swayne, J.).

58. I have written on this topic in *David's Hammer: The Case for an Activist Judiciary* (Washington, DC: Cato Institute, 2007).

59. Robert H. Bork, *The Tempting of America: The Political Seduction of the Law* (New York: Free Press, 1990), pp. 37–39.

60. Bork, *The Tempting of America*, p. 166.

61. Quoted in Labbe and Lurie, *The Slaughterhouse Cases*, p.2.

62. *Slaughter-House*, 83 U.S. at 130 (Swayne, J.).

63. 163 U.S. 537 (1896).

64. I write about this evolution in greater detail in *The Affirmative Action Fraud: Can We Restore the American Civil Rights Vision?* (Washington, DC: Cato Institute, 1996).

65. Curtis, *No State Shall Abridge*, p. 175.

66. Clarence Thomas, "The Higher Law Background of the Privileges or Immunities Clause of the Fourteenth Amendment," 12 *Harvard Journal of Law and Public Policy* 63, 64 (1989).

Part 3: The Aftermath of Slaughter-House

1. *Slaughter-House*, 83 U.S. at 79.

2. Labbe and Lurie, *The Slaughterhouse Cases*, p. 7.

3. An excellent recounting of the laws and jurisprudence of this period, including an analysis of the nature, scope, and devastating impact of economic regulations on blacks, is provided in David E. Bernstein, *Only One Place of Redress: African Americans, Labor Regulations, & The Courts from Reconstruction to the New Deal* (Durham, NC: Duke University Press, 2001).

4. Cong. Globe, 43rd Cong., 1st Sess., 1874, S. p. 4148.

5. Quoted in Curtis, *No State Shall Abridge*, p. 177.

6. See generally Curtis, *No State Shall Abridge*, pp. 177–78; Clint Bolick, *Unfinished Business: A Civil Rights Strategy for America's Third Century* (San Francisco, CA: Pacific Research Institute, 1990), p. 69.

7. *Bradwell v. The State*, 83 U.S. 130, 139 (1873).

8. *Bradwell*, 83 U.S. at 140 (Bradley, J., concurring).

9. *Bradwell*, 83 U.S. at 141 (Bradley, J.).

10. This history is taken from *McDonald*, p. 9 (majority) and 4 (Thomas, J.).

11. *U.S. v. Cruikshank*, 92 U.S. 542, 551 (1875).

12. Bolick, *Unfinished Business*, p. 69.

13. Bolick, *Unfinished Business*, p. 70.

14. Shankman and Pilon, "Reviving the Privileges or Immunities Clause," p. 41.

15. Cong. Globe, 39th Cong., 1st Sess., 1866, S. p. 2765.

16. Cong. Globe, 39th Cong., 1st Sess., 1866, S. p. 65.

17. Lofgren, *The Plessy Case*, p. 32.

18. Lofgren, *The Plessy Case*, p. 41.

19. *Plessy v. Ferguson*, 163 U.S. 537, 544 (1896).

20. *Plessy*, 163 U.S. at 563 (Harlan, J., dissenting).

21. *Plessy*, 163 U.S. at 559 (Harlan, J.).

22. *Berea College v. Kentucky*, 211 U.S. 45, 67 (1908) (Harlan, J., dissenting).

23. For an excellent discussion of the jurisprudence of this period, see Sandefur, *The Right to Earn a Living*, pp. 90–107.

24. *Munn v. Illinois*, 94 U.S. 113, 126 (1876).

25. *Munn*, 94 U.S. at 138–40 (Field, J., dissenting).

26. *Allgeyer v. Louisiana*, 165 U.S. 578, 589 (1897).

27. *Yick Wo v. Hopkins*, 118 U.S. 356, 370 (1886).

28. See Sandefur, *The Right to Earn a Living*, pp. 103–04.

29. *Lochner v. New York*, 198 U.S. 45, 56 (1905).

30. *Id.*, 198 U.S. at 53.

31. *Id.*, 198 U.S. at 64.

32. *Id.*, 198 U.S. at 59.

33. *Id.*, 198 U.S. at 57.

34. *Id.*, 198 U.S. at 56.

35. *Id.*, 198 U.S. at 65–66 (Harlan, J., dissenting) (citation omitted).

36. *Id.*, 198 U.S. at 69 (Harlan, J.).

37. *Id.*, 198 U.S. at 75 (Holmes, J., dissenting).

38. *Id.*, 198 U.S. at 75–76 (Holmes, J.).

39. Sandefur, *The Right to Earn a Living*, p. 127 (citation omitted).

40. *Nebbia v. New York*, 291 U.S. 502, 537 (1934).

41. *Adkins v. Children's Hospital*, 261 U.S. 525 (1923).

42. *West Coast Hotel Co. v. Parrish*, 300 U.S. 379, 391 (1937). Actually, it does. Article I, section 10, clause 1 of the Constitution provides, "No State shall . . . pass any law . . . impairing the Obligation of Contracts . . ." This provision is known as the Contract Clause.

43. *Id.*, 300 U.S. at 394.

44. *Id.*, 300 U.S. at 399.

45. *Id.*, 300 U.S. at 399–400.

46. *Id.*, 300 U.S. at 402 (Sutherland, J., dissenting).

47. *Id.*, 300 U.S. at 413 (Sutherland, J.).

48. *Id.*, 300 U.S. at 406 (Sutherland, J.).

49. *Colgate v. Harvey*, 296 U.S. 404, 431 (1935).

50. *Colgate*, 296 U.S. at 433.

51. *Colgate*, 296 U.S. at 444 (Stone, J., dissenting in part).

52. *Colgate*, 296 U.S. at 445–46 (Stone, J.).

53. *Madden v. Commonwealth of Kentucky*, 309 U.S. 83, 88 (1940).

54. *Madden*, 309 U.S. at 92–93.

55. *United States v. Carolene Products Co.*, 304 U.S. 144 (1938).

56. *Carolene Products*, 304 U.S. at 152 n. 4.

57. *Home Building & Loan Association v. Blaisdell*, 290 U.S. 398 (1934).

58. *Berman v. Parker*, 348 U.S. 26, 33 (1954).

59. *Kelo v. City of New London*, 545 U.S. 469 (2005).

60. A compelling rendition of this tragic story is presented in Jeff Benedict, *Little Pink House: A True Story of Defiance and Courage* (New York: Grand Central Publishing, 2009).

61. *Wickard v. Filburn*, 317 U.S. 111 (1942).

62. Many of the cases discussed in this section are examined in greater detail in two outstanding books, Robert A. Levy and William Mellor, *The Dirty Dozen: How Twelve Supreme Court Cases Radically Expanded Government and Eroded Freedom* (New York: Sentinel, 2008); and Richard A. Epstein, *How Progressives Rewrote the Constitution* (Washington, DC: Cato Institute, 2006).

63. See Clint Bolick, *David's Hammer: The Case for an Activist Judiciary* (Washington, DC: Cato Institute, 2007), pp. 83–85 and 121–23.

64. Shankman and Pilon, "Reviving the Privileges or Immunities Clause," p. 40.

Part 4: A Rebirth for Economic Liberty

1. Bernard H. Siegan, *Economic Liberties and the Constitution* (Chicago: University of Chicago Press, 1981).

2. Richard A. Epstein, *Takings: Private Property and the Power of Eminent Domain* (Cambridge, MA: 1985).

3. See, e.g., Randy E. Barnett, *Restoring the Lost Constitution: The Presumption of Liberty* (Princeton, NJ: Princeton University Press, 2004).

4. See, e.g., Ann Southworth, *Lawyers of the Right: Professionalizing the Conservative Coalition* (Chicago: University of Chicago Press, 2008).

5. *City of Cleburne v. Cleburne Living Center*, 473 U.S. 432, 439 (1985).

6. *Id.*, 473 U.S. at 441, 443, and 449.

7. *Moore v. City of East Cleveland*, 431 U.S. 494, 499 (1977) (plurality).

8. *Id.*, 431 U.S. at 500 (plurality).

9. *Id.*, 431 U.S. at 502 (plurality) (quoting *Poe v. Ullman*, 367 U.S. 497, 543 (1961) (Harlan, J., dissenting).

10. *Id.*, 431 U.S. at 503 (plurality) (citation omitted).

11. *United Building & Construction Trades Council of Camden County and Vicinity v. Mayor and Council of City of Camden*, 465 U.S. 208, 219 (1984).

12. *Brown v. Barry*, 710 F. Supp. 352, 355 (D.D.C. 1989) (emphasis in original).

13. *Id.*, 710 F. Supp. at 356.

14. *Santos v. City of Houston*, 852 F. Supp. 601, 608 (S.D. Tex. 1994).

15. See Bolick, *David's Hammer*, pp. 106–07.

16. See Bolick, *David's Hammer*, pp. 97–98.

17. *Cornwell v. Hamilton*, 80 F. Supp. 2d 1101, 1106 (S. D. Cal. 1999).

18. *Craigmiles v. Giles*, 312 F.3d 220, 228 (6th Cir. 2002).

19. *Id.*, 312 F.3d at 229.

20. *Powers v. Harris*, 379 F.3d 1208, 1220 (10th Cir. 2004).

21. *Id.*, 379 F.3d at 1221–22.

22. Sandefur, *The Right to Earn a Living*, p. 157 (emphasis in original).

23. *Merrifield v. Lockyer*, 547 F.3d 978, 991 n.15 (9th Cir. 2008).

24. Jennifer Levitz, "Coffins Made With Brotherly Love Have Undertakers Throwing Dirt," *Wall Street Journal* (Aug. 25, 2010), pp. A1 and A12.

25. *Saenz v. Roe*, 526 U.S. 489, 502 (1999).

26. *Id.*, 526 U.S. at 504.

27. *Id.*, 526 U.S. at 521 (Thomas, J., dissenting).

28. *Id.*, 526 U.S. at 522 & n.1 (Thomas, J.).

29. *Id.*, 526 U.S. at 527–28 (Thomas, J.).

30. *District of Columbia v. Heller*, 128 S.Ct. 2783 (2008).

31. Transcript of Oral Argument, *McDonald v. City of Chicago*, No. 08–1521 (March 2, 2010), pp. 3–11.

32. *McDonald v. City of Chicago*, No. 08–1521, slip op. (June 28, 2010) at 6 (majority).

33. *Id.*, slip op. at 8. Among the scholars cited for that consensus is Yale Law Professor Akhil Amar, who wrote that "[v]irtually no serious modern scholar—left, right, and center—thinks that this [interpretation of the privileges or immunities clause in *Slaughter-House*] is a plausible reading of the Amendment." Akhil Amar, "Substance and Method in the Year 2000," 28 *Pepperdine Law Review* 601, 631 n.178 (2001).

34. *McDonald*, slip op. at 10 (plurality).

35. *Id.*, slip op. at 1 (Thomas, J., concurring in part and concurring in the judgment).

36. *Id.*, slip op. at 47 (Thomas, J.).

37. *Id.*, slip op. at 52 (Thomas, J.).

38. See, e.g., *Romer v. Evans*, 517 U.S. 620 (1996).

39. For a discussion of prospects and strategies for state constitutional litigation, see Bolick, *David's Hammer*, pp. 139–55; see also Clint Bolick, "Brennan's Epiphany: The Necessity of Invoking State Constitutions to Protect Freedom," 12 *Texas Review of Law & Politics* 137 (2007).

40. See, e.g., *State v. Cromwell*, 9 N.W.2d 914 (N.D. 1943) and *Buehman v. Bechtel*, 114 P.2d 227 (Ariz. 1941), both striking down photography regulations.

41. I am grateful to my former Institute for Justice colleague Tim Keller for referring this case to me.

■ ABOUT THE AUTHOR

Clint Bolick is one of America's premier constitutional litigators, having won U.S. Supreme Court decisions on school vouchers and the direct interstate shipment of wine to consumers and numerous other precedent-setting cases in federal and state courts around the nation. *Legal Times* named him one of the ninety greatest DC lawyers of the past thirty years; *American Lawyer* named him one of three lawyers of the year in 2003; and he was a recipient of the Bradley Prize. Bolick heads the Goldwater Institute's Scharf-Norton Center for Constitutional Litigation in Phoenix and serves as a research fellow for the Hoover Institution. He is the author of several books; his most recent title is *David's Hammer: The Case for an Activist Judiciary*.

▌ INDEX